LIVING AT HIGH NOON

Gordon MacDonald

LIVING AT HIGH NOON

Reflections on the Dramas of Mid-Life

CARMEL • NEW YORK 10512

This Guideposts edition is published by
special arrangement with Fleming H. Revell Company

Library of Congress Cataloging in Publication Data

MacDonald, Gordon.
   Living at high noon.

   1. Middle age—Religious life.
I. Title.
BV4579.5.M3   1985   248.8'4   84-17802
ISBN 0-8007-1240-4

Contents

6   *CONTENTS*

Section V: Reflections on Mid-Life Spirituality

Introduction
Facing Life at High Noon

I'm hardly alone in my thoughts and attitudes toward mid-life. Most of us don't quite know how to handle the inescapable changes that seem to fill all areas of our lives.

On the day I write this introduction I am forty-five years old. I think I like being forty-five, but I'm not sure. My opinion changes regularly.

I like being forty-five when I face people and situations I know I couldn't have handled fifteen years ago. Then I'm excited about the accumulation of experience and wisdom time has brought me.

I do not like being forty-five when bright young men and pretty young ladies ignore me and make it obvious that they consider me over the hill, a mere father figure. And I do not like being forty-five when it occasionally dawns on me that I have about twenty-five to thirty working years left, and I'm not overjoyed about how much I have accomplished during the first twenty-five years.

On the other hand, at forty-five fewer people try to hustle me into buying products I do not want. I also find it easier to say no to things I don't want to do. Knowing my capabilities and my limits, I tend to make a fool out of myself less frequently than before. These are certainly assets that more than compensate for the image of forty-five.

Yet my body tends toward occasional rebellion: tired eyes, aching muscles, and a stomach that growls within and overhangs without when inordinately filled. So, you see, I'm reluctant to form a final opinion on forty-five. I suspect I'll be more positive about it when I'm forty-seven.

Some years ago I began to get hints that this up-and-down love-hate relationship with mid-life was going to cause a potentially uncomfortable period in my life. In fact I came to realize that I could guarantee the discomfort, if I didn't make some preparations. So I began to do just that.

I listened to people talk about this time of life. I read the available literature. And I began to formulate some theories. Finally, I hit the big "four-oh" and started through the first phases of mid-life itself.

Someone once said to me, "I started out the ball game of life intent on hitting a home run every time I came to bat. Now I'm in the sixth inning of my life game, and all I want to do is get through the 'game' without being beaned." That statement began to have meaning.

Well, I'm forty-five and in the fifth or sixth inning, I think. I'm still out trying to hit home runs. But I must admit, in keeping with my friend's metaphor, that I'm now a bit more respectful of the pitcher on the mound, because he does seem a bit wild at times.

So here I am writing a book at middle life. Some call it midlife, others middlesence. Karl Jung called it the noon of life, and I'm drawn to his words. Thus *Living at High Noon.* That's where I am, and that's where millions of "war babies" are. We are living at high noon. Some of us are enjoying the experience.

When I decided to write about living at high noon, I realized I could not write as one who has seen it all. Perhaps I'd be more qualified on that basis when I reach the eighth inning or (switching to Jung's metaphor) the twilight hours. And I cannot write as a researcher with a huge data base derived from hundreds of laboratory experiments resulting from testing and interviews. My data is mere observation and experience. But I can write more or less as a philosopher, as a pastor who is a student of people, as a man who likes to think about what he is seeing and feeling.

I've written a bit about myself in this book, where I thought it might be useful. And I've written about others whom I've come to know and have been willing to share their insights and experiences with me. Occasionally there are those "composite" characters who are not necessarily real but who are, on the other hand, certainly realistic.

It seems to me that in writing *Living at High Noon,* I took some risks that I might be guilty of asking more questions than of providing answers. But perhaps that is because there are many mysteries to mid-life, and so many varieties of mid-life exist that one could hardly mount an all-encompassing response to everything with which those in the noon of life are living. But I would be quite content if the reader were to identify with the questions and the observations and then wrestle along with me day by day toward the honest answers.

This is not a theological book, but one Christian in orientation, committed to the notion that at the root of all phases of life a healthy spiritual perspective is an absolute necessity. Middle life without an awareness of intimacy with God is to me a troubling matter.

And that is in part what *Living at High Noon* is all about—a walk through what I see to be the great themes of the afternoon of life: my physical body, my vocation, my relationships, and my spirit. That's me—all forty-five years of me. Join me in my living at high noon and see if we're sharing similar thoughts, reactions, and feelings.

I'd probably never have attempted to record this description of life at high noon if it hadn't been for some special people around me. My wife, Gail, of course, who talks through each of my books with me and is the first to tell me when my words are mere empty drivel. But she quickly affirms the insights worth polishing, and for that I am profoundly thankful.

There are a host of people who make up my world in Lexington, Massachusetts: associates in the pastoral ministry and in lay leadership. They graciously listen to me preach; they patiently follow my sophomoric leadership; and they gently offer the needed critique when I come at them, as it is said, "off the wall." May they be blessed forever.

We're not ready for rocking chairs yet, but at forty-five, while the noontime sun is high and hot, a park bench would be a welcome sight. Perhaps we could sit there and do our reflecting on what it means to engage in living at high noon.

Section I

Reflections on the Mid-Life Reality

1
Not Exactly Superstars

I recall a hot, humid summer evening, when along with a few hundred others, I sat in a gymnasium, waiting for the beginning of an annual basketball game between teams of guests and staffers at a vacation resort. It was a big night for everyone. Across the acres of this vacationland, everything ground to a halt. There were no meetings in progress; no couples had slipped away for a moonlight swim or a romantic canoe ride. Apparently the action on the basketball court was far too important for anyone to miss.

All the ornaments of athletic competition garbed the gym. It seemed as if we were at Madison Square Garden watching a college championship game. Uniformed players practiced their lay-up shots; the scoring officials sat at the mid-court table, making the last pregame checks of their record books. And the striped-shirt referees stood nervously at the jump-ball circle, ready to whistle the game into motion.

The game began, and the two teams raced back and forth from hoop to hoop, an occasional shot actually dropping through for a score. The crowd screamed; the pep band played; and the scoreboard blinked alive with lights, reflecting the points, the fouls, and the time remaining. But in the middle of it all, I strangely found myself gradually losing interest in basketball. Does it make sense to say that I stopped watching players and spectators and started looking at persons? What I think I saw moved me to the belief that the encounter between two teams of athletes was more than just a game.

My initial interest centered on the team of "staffers"—the fellows who maintained the camp grounds and served tables at meals. This collection of high school and college boys played with the usual vigor and skill of youth. They obviously wanted to win, for to triumph on any occasion when the opponents were certified adults meant to establish superiority over—or at least equality with—an older generation. I could understand the importance to them that they prove over and over again that they were *men*. There is nothing novel or modern about that concern. I would have expected it from them at any time.

But I found the other team much more fascinating: the guests, a collection of males ranging in age from their late twenties to the early forties. Perhaps they will not feel overly offended if I confess that as I watched them play, they reminded me of automobile tires that have accumulated about 20,000 miles of road wear. The symptoms? Shortness of breath, receding hairlines, and sagging stomachs. It probably isn't necessary to extend the list beyond that. To say the least, they did not exactly look like superstars.

The intensity of their play prompted my curiosity to range beyond the limits of the game. Were members of the guest team revealing anything when they frequently questioned the referee's judgment, grimaced at each error committed by their puffing teammates, and reverted to childlike enthusiasm at the scoring of every friendly point?

Add to the intensity a suspicion about nostalgia. Could some in that gymnasium unconsciously be attempting to re-create something of the "good old days," when life seemed far less complicated than the ulcers, the commuter traffic, and the 1040 forms of adult life? Some men and women might remember moments when young people competed for the glory of their school, the admiration of their romantic idols, and the satisfaction of being the best among peers.

Did nostalgia grip a few spectators in the grandstands? Could it underlie the frenzied cheering mounted by the players' wives? Could part of all this enthusiasm actually be a kind of reverie that recalled days when life was much less overloaded with obligation, responsibility, and bone-wearying schedules?

Clearly winning held just as much importance for this hard-breathing, sweating team of stockbrokers, salesmen, and engineers as it did for the kids on the other side. And one could not escape the fact that it was just as important up there in the grandstands. Why?

What could a superior score prove? Why would grown men of thirty-eight feel they had to match and even best the skill, the stamina, and the strength of boys barely nineteen and twenty? What composes the internal force that causes a man, headed toward middle years of life, to risk dignity, self-image, bones, and muscles, and sometimes even friendships? Did the intensity of play, the evident emotion of nostalgia, have something to do with an urgency to prove that people of middle adult years are really still young? That speculative question admitted almost no hope of a measurable answer. But I confess my suspicions.

Did a parallel exist between the behavior of these people and the tragic, sudden urge of a man to leave a wife of twenty years for a younger, more attractive lover? Might that game parallel in emotion those moments when a man or woman drifts into the college-age shop of a clothing store to select styles more aptly befitting someone two decades his or her junior?

To be seen with the young, to dress like the young, to compete with the young—does a message weave its way through such pursuits? And does that message suggest that many people fear the possibility of losing their youth? For not to be young somehow seems to indicate that one is old. And all too often the logic of our culture suggests that growing old is strangely indecent or obscene. These ponderous thoughts seemed filled with devastating implications. They hardly belonged at a basketball game. But I could not squelch their force. Thus my brooding continued, an uneasiness about my conclusions growing.

Looking back now upon that game, I remember a revealing study of certain faces. I kept thinking that I'd seen some of the same expressions on other occasions. One face, for example, plainly exhibited exhaustion. I recalled the same patterns in the expression of a man who had gone through a recent experience of failure in relationship with his rebellious teenager. He had not wanted to admit defeat, but his energy of love had taken him as far as he could go. Like a fatigued basketball player, he had no alternative but to sit down on the bench and ponder a long and apparently losing effort as a father.

A second face in the gym mirrored frustration when an older player found that he simply could not outrun or outmaneuver his smaller and younger opponent. Obviously in the beginning moments he anticipated showing this young smart aleck how to play the game. But now, instead of teaching, he learned. As I watched him and reminded myself that it was just a game, I could not ignore the fact that I'd seen that same frustration in another situation: a man who wears travel-knit suits, hangs on frantically to a job he can hardly master, tries to drop a few names of top people he's met in the business community, but all the time quietly knows (but can't face) that he is steadily losing ground to young competitors for his present job and future advancement.

A third face now in the crowd: the hard lines of envy about the mouth and eyes of a player's wife as she watches the agile and enthusiastic choreography of a young camp-staff girl who acts as a cheerleader. Did the expressions betray the existence of comparisons going on somewhere in the heart? Perhaps she contemplated the differences in their contrasting weight and shape. Was that fair to herself, after having become mother to three children? Did she covet the younger woman's seemingly endless energy? Could she have wistfully recalled the mystery of those moments when one anticipated an after-game date? The cheerleader's perpetual vigor may have done nothing but accentuate the numbing feeling of tiredness that seemed to bring many middle-aged days to their conclusions.

As I recall that game a question flashes across my mind. It moves straight as a laser beam to the center of my being, with its chilling accusation. Had I been doing something similar to what the psychologist calls projection? Could I have read into the actions and expressions of others something only too real within me? Were the exhaustion, the envy, the frustration part of *my* innermost being?

The finger of suspicion slowly turns to where it should have been in the first place: upon myself. Painfully I inwardly ask if I had been a good enough athlete, wouldn't I have enjoyed a starting position on that team, where I could have proved that my middle-aged legs were as capable as they once were when I ran the quarter mile in competitive time? A brutal question to self—could the impossible dream of recapturing the moment of former times when brute strength won high recognition have consumed me?

I alternatively smile and frown: a smile for the inner subtlety of my own thoughts, a frown that such issues really exist within me. I learn something about myself that I had perhaps resisted in previous thought. I, too, am growing old, and something within me feels slightly uncomfortable with the idea. What I think I see as resistance in others may also take place within myself. I am just like them; in fact, I may even be worse.

Why should one feel uneasy about this matter of growing old? Why do we instinctively pursue the fantasies of youth? I resolved in that moment, as I remembered the hot gymnasium, to find out the answer, and in those moments I gave literary birth to a chain of mid-life confessions.

I find it interesting that even a basketball game can bring to the surface those common emotions of the great issues of living. In a game compressed into forty-eight minutes, one can see many classic themes of human existence as people strain toward the objectives of individual and team success. Out on the floor, the struggles of competition, winning, losing, exer-

tion and exhaustion, leadership, humiliation, and final judgment take place. The issues seem black and white in the middle
of a game; they are observable and measurable. Not so in the
routine of living, however.

But hidden or revealed, we consistently feel the effects of
these issues as we face relentless tests as to what kind of human
beings we are. At the end of the game, we all exited from the
gym, to grapple with the same issues, but on a level of reality
with much more significant results. Maybe the player's wife
who had been watching the cheerleader sensed this. Perhaps
after the earlier disquieting moments, she dismissed the unfair
conclusions of her surface comparisons by saying to herself,
Drat it, what does that kid know about life anyway? If she did
indeed say that, the older woman had recognized once again
the larger, the more real game, with its greater stakes; she lives
in it every day. But still for just a moment, perhaps it would
have been nice to have exchanged places with the carefree,
bouncing teenager. At least that's what I suspect she may have
been thinking.

Later on I would discover that these primitive thoughts in a
grandstand were neither profound nor unique. As one psychologist would later say to me, "Gordon, when you notice those
things and think those thoughts, you're right on schedule.
Don't you realize that those are the kind of ideas a man in his
late thirties would nurse along?"

When I wondered aloud what he meant by "right on schedule" and "kinds of thoughts," he responded, "Welcome to the
world of adult development. You won't believe what you're
going to find."

He was right! The depth of discovery has been unbelievable,
sometimes frightening, but, nevertheless, exciting. You and I
might call it growing old. The student of personality prefers to
call it adult development. His phrase seems far less threatening, for this moment at least, until we come later to the hopeful
conclusion: Growing old is not bad, not weakening, and not to
be feared.

Only in recent years have people begun to give serious attention to the phases through which adults move in the process of living. We know a lot about the development of children and adolescents. Most scholarly attention has centered in the early years of life, because it seemed obvious that adults were the products of the sum total of choices and circumstances created in the preadult period. Adults were finished products, we assumed. They had financial problems, career problems, time-use problems, relational problems. But internally adults were adults. They had finished developing. Not so!

Perhaps the great European psychiatrist Carl Jung first started the change in such thinking. In one of his greatest literary works, *Modern Man in Search of a Soul* (actually a compilation of several lectures), Jung included an essay entitled "The Stages of Life." He attempted to demonstrate the flow of human development from birth to death. This process, he said, can be divided up into four quarters or phases: childhood, youth–young adult, mid-life, and old age. More illustratively, he recalls the passage of the sun from the east to the west, suggesting that one might compare the stages of life to the solar crossing of the sky.

All these corresponding segments meant that Carl Jung saw that a person at the age of thirty-five to fifty was at the "noon" of life. *High noon!* At this center line, life reached a dramatic point of intensity. During the ascent period (the morning hours), Jung suggested that a person tends to be preoccupied with positioning himself in the society around him. The dominant themes include the development of marriage, the formation of a career, the raising of children, the crystallizing of a whole personality. These Jung saw as the pursuit of *nature.*

The descent period, Jung suggested, should center its attention on other things. If matters of nature asserted themselves in the "morning" of life, then matters of *culture* should emerge as the central themes in the afternoon of life. The pursuit of culture means a transition to a more contemplative style of life. It hints at the possibility of one's beginning to spend time perceiving, evaluating, enjoying, and creating with the "stuff" of the world about him. If people did not tend to be so fearful of the aging process, what Jung proposes in the pursuit of culture could sound exciting.

A careful reading of Jung's essay shows that he felt deeply concerned about the events that occurred around noon. He warned that during this period of life dramatic changes would probably take place. Changes in character, in habit patterns, and even in convictions. These changes could come about through repudiation of the past years, or they might even happen as one reached back into his childhood and recovered patterns of behavior suspended during the adolescent and young-adult period.

What bothered Carl Jung most of all, it seems, was that he saw very few people prepared to face the noon of life. I think I hear him warning the reader of an "ambush" at high noon, which can be destructive if not anticipated.

Having given a brief description of some kinds of changes that one can expect at mid-life, Jung laments that many middle-agers are "wholly unprepared as they embark upon the second half of life." Jung goes on to say:

> We take this step with the false presupposition that our truths and ideals will serve us hitherto. But we cannot live the afternoon of life according to the program of life's morning—for what was great in the morning will be little at evening, and what in the morning was true will at evening have become a lie. I have given psychological treatment to too many people of advancing years, and have looked too often into the secret chambers of their souls, not to be moved by this fundamental truth.

What's Jung saying? Change marks mid-life, but few people—if any—prepare themselves for the changes. They think to cross from the morning to afternoon using the values and convictions of the past. But Jung claims that it cannot normally be done. Noon can become a triumphant experience *only for those who have prepared for its inevitable coming.* But most people, I hear him saying, have no preparation.

My experience in working with people as a pastor supports the things that Carl Jung points out. Anyone who befriends people in crisis will observe the lack of readiness of most men and women to face each stage of life. "Why didn't someone tell me this was going to happen?" is a frequent question.

Perhaps we so easily become preoccupied with the present, we resist preparing for the future. I see this in the majority of the young couples who come asking me to officiate at their wedding ceremonies. They show little, if any, interest in proffered premarital counseling, supposing that the romance of the present is strong enough to gird them for the challenges of the future. It does not seem to occur to them that there will be external and internal changes of a significant nature when they commit themselves to each other in a more formal way.

I sense the same pattern of disinterest—or is it avoidance?—in many people living in the later hours of the morning of their lives. They shield their eyes from the realities of noon. Either from ignorance or design, they choose not to think about the transitions that will happen at mid-life. And in making that choice they set themselves up for the noontime ambush of change, which will most certainly come.

As I look back upon the conversations I have had in my office, I begin to realize how many of them centered on the matters of mid-life. Men and women have come to talk about hurts, aches, confusions, resentments that were, on many occasions, simply mid-life ambushes. What they saw as problems in a larger sense formed part of a process of transition from morning to afternoon. If they could have only been warned and prepared ahead of time! But if the warnings had been sounded, would they have listened or simply imagined that the caution signals rang for everyone else?

Most would not have had a mind to listen. A typical young

mother has no time or desire to think about future life, when her children will have left home. A career person does not wish to contemplate possible reactions when, someday, it becomes apparent that one has reached the extent of his or her vocational capacities. A man does not think it necessary to ask whether the underlying values of his life-style will stand the shocks of the sudden deaths of friends and relatives he loves. A woman hopes she can put off the inevitable menopause as long as possible; she thinks of it as her enemy, and she resents its growing shadow.

My own interest in the mid-life experience introduced me to a new vocabulary. The predominant word used by writers and thinkers in adult development is *crisis*, and the phrase *mid-life crisis* quickly becomes a familiar term. When author Eda LeShan wrote about mid-life, she attempted to put a positive emphasis in her writing and thus entitled her book *The* Wonderful *Crisis of Middle Age*. In 1976 Gail Sheehy wrote about the broader characteristics of adult development. But she resented the negative implications of the word *crisis* and chose the word *passages,* so as to portray the growing adult as moving through a series of gateways, each providing new choices and new consequences.

I prefer the word *drama*. A drama can be a series of large or small events that confront a person with the potential of change. The whole of mid-life is a drama, but within the drama several subdramas move side by side. At times they dovetail; on other occasions the subdramas move at different speeds toward divergent objectives. But each of them etches out upon the spirit of a person a new identity and a new perception of life. When the dramas of mid-life have been completed, no one remains as he was before the dramas began.

Many of us already face the dramas of high noon. But many more remain in that period just before the noon hour strikes. Those of us already at the magic hour may yet have time to think through our role in each of the acts. For those approaching high noon, time may still exist to chart the obstacles and opportunities and prepare for the challenges. One sure thing: There will be dramas. The only uncertainty lies in the conclusions of the final acts.

For most of us the events of mid-life begin before Carl Jung's "noon" and will continue into the early afternoon hours. There would be no point in trying to identify specific ages when dramas either begin or end—better to sort out the major themes and their implications. My own thinking has brought me to suggest that four personal dramas take center stage at high noon, each real, unique, and unavoidable. Woven among these four, a thousand subdramas play across our lives, all rooted in the four that most generally mark high noon.

The first is that of *living*. This theme grows out of natural changes within our bodies. Physiological systems make significant shifts at high noon. Some physical components within us will slow down. Others even cease to operate. Here and there pieces and sections of us will suddenly grow or shrink. It can be a potentially frightening experience for the uninformed. Our capacity to cope with our physiological changes in a large part determines our health in the afternoon hours of life. In a world overwhelmed with information about ourselves, startlingly few people know or care about the physiological changes they face.

A second drama of high noon is that of *knowing*. Call it the drama of changing relationships. Our marriages, our friendships, our children, and our parents will probably all change on us to some extent at mid-life. Some of them leave us through death, rebellion, or the call of stronger priorities. Almost none of these changes prove uncomplicated. They certainly do not come without some kind of pain.

A third drama is that of *doing*, and here we focus on the matter of vocation. I use the word *vocation* to describe the things we do in life in the pursuit of career. At high noon most of us first face the facts of failure or success. For the first time we begin to determine whether or not we made right choices at an earlier age. At mid-life we make a new measurement as to just how important our vocation is to us in the light of other priorities. Almost no one avoids some kind of vocational drama.

A final high-noon drama of personal belief may be the most important, although the least measurable. How do believing and its correlated act, commitment—presumably the highest acts of a human being—survive the realities of high noon? Almost every mid-lifer has enough evidence to make drastic decisions about his or her value structure. Almost all make new choices about the foundational aspects of their inner spirits at mid-life. For some, high noon brings a sense of disillusionment about belief, a feeling of being let down. For others, beliefs accelerate. When the drama of believing at high noon ends, a new and different person will probably exist.

Many have said, "Life begins at forty," but few have actually wanted to believe it. Telltale messages pass back and forth when people kid about entering middle age. For years Americans laughed with Jack Benny as he insisted on remaining thirty-nine years old. We laughed because not to have laughed would have made it necessary to face the fact that forty was coming inexorably closer. For many people, not to have laughed would have been to cry. Few people want to admit to middle age. Somehow it seems that in middle age one simply stops growing.

Eda LeShan urgently warns against such thinking (*italics mine*):

> It may seem strange, but I believe deeply that for those of us who are middle aged *the most profound growing still lies ahead of us.* We are a generation which has been brain washed into believing that genuine growing is something that takes place only during one's childhood. In the admittedly fascinating pre-occupation of recent years with the "ages and stages" of childhood, we have all but ignored the fact that growing and learning and changing are never

(not even mostly) the prerogative of childhood; quite the contrary—*what happens to us after the age of twenty-one is just as significant, just as dramatic, as anything that has happened before.*

Eda LeShan is not an unreal optimist. She puts her finger on one of the great acts of God in creation. Living things are created to grow, to change, to produce. In every stage, they take on new color, new strengths, and new capacities. Nowhere can that prove more true than in the mid-life period. LeShan takes an offensive position just when most people move on to the defense. She has a sound idea.

My mind does another slow-motion instant replay of that night, near the end of the basketball game. Both sides, soaked with the sweat generated during the intense moments of intergenerational rivalry, have clearly accepted that the guests—the older men—will lose. At first they had surged ahead on the benefits of years of athletic experience. But by the middle of the game, the young men's stamina began to assert itself as a key factor. In terms of scoring the game actually finished by the beginning of the fourth quarter.

The older men now feel exhausted. They look frequently toward the clock, and one gets the impression that they would like to hurry the game along. The fatigue and the losing score both conspire to erase former smiles of confidence.

As I sit in my mental grandstand, I continue in my philosophical mood. I find myself wishing that someone could halt this game and move among these defeated men, telling them that winning by the numbers is not that important. It wouldn't have proved anything substantial if they could have brought home the victory. If they had won, it would have only been a temporary demonstration, and the cruel irony would have been that tomorrow would have brought another in the unending challenges between the generations. Sooner or later they would lose. The longer they postpone the inevitable loss, the more painful its reality when it arrives.

I remember that when the scoreboard horn sounded the end of the game, the people in the gym erupted in a final salute to the victors. Then they hurried on out for a late-evening snack, content with the fact that they'd seen a great basketball game. Everyone felt satisfied.

But I had found myself headed toward the place where I would sleep that night. I wanted to think about the dramas of high noon more than to linger over an ice cream sundae, talking about somebody's breakaway shot. I wanted to think about the dramas because I was growing more and more certain that they are packed with great opportunity for growth and maturity.

But I cannot escape the irony that the high-noon dramas that can lead to opportunity actually cause many people psychic aches and pains from which they may never recover. *Almost always the difference between the positive and the negative, growing or shriveling, is determined by the preparation and information made and possessed by the mid-life person.*

The negative result? People feeling alone, bitter, betrayed, disillusioned. Does someone need to blow the whistle in the game of life and tell such men and women that it can be okay? That they can receive some good news?

And where might one begin? Perhaps by saying that one need never face the dramas of high noon alone. Perhaps by pointing to a God who wishes to walk alongside, gently disclosing new and special ways of continuing life's growing process. God's way provides opportunity; other ways all too often stumble amongst the obstacles. Come to the dramas, come at high noon. For those who have the courage to ponder and prepare, there awaits an experience of special joy. One need not look back; a wholeness of life lies just ahead.

2
Life at Half-mast

When I see a flag flying at half-mast, I immediately sense distress. Lowered to the halfway point on a pole, the flag's position signals death, loss, grief. I most frequently see something like that at the Lexington battlegreen, which I pass early each morning on the way to my study.

The green is the site of one of the first open conflicts in America's Revolutionary War. High above the battle monuments and the beautiful trees, a large American flag whips in the New England breeze. It remains there day and night. But sometimes the flag stands not at the top of the pole, but halfway down, and that indicates that life has ended for some prominent person in our nation.

That's exactly where the flag is one morning when I walk toward the Pewter Pot (our local coffee-and-roll shop) for a breakfast with a man who had called and asked if we could have a talk.

"What's happening to me?" he asks after we take our places at a corner table. He springs the question after some small talk about last night's presidential press conference, today's weather, and the restaurant.

Confident that I am in a receptive mood, he begins to describe a struggle he thinks unique, slightly embarrassing, and probably indicative of personal failure. As he talks, I listen, trying very hard not to jump to premature conclusions. But I can't help thinking that he is simply pointing to one more version of the high-noon dramas. He seems to wrestle with vocation and relationship. What I call drama, he calls disaster.

Looking back across his life, my friend speaks nostalgically of an exciting career with a future. At least that's what it was when he started: a career. But now he calls it simply a job, and he labels his work a bore. An encouraging nod of my head here and there pushes him on in his story. Fifteen years ago, he thinks out loud, he would have given his right arm to do what he does today. But now that he has achieved most of his professional goal, he finds the pursuit increasingly tasteless. "Don't misunderstand," he says, "I'm not looking for money. At this point, I'm not even interested in a promotion. Do you know what I mean?"

I think I understand; so I say so, and he moves on.

"I don't enjoy working as hard as I used to. No new goals seem to interest me or motivate me. I feel as if I'm just putting in time."

We pause at this and talk a little about mental fatigue, boredom, and sameness, and I assure him, at least for the moment, that he is not living with a strange or peculiar feeling. Growing more obviously confident about my acceptance of him with his supposed flaws and struggles, he suddenly changes the subject of work and introduces another troubled side of his life.

"That's not the only thing plaguing me," he says. "To be perfectly frank with you, I feel the same way about my marriage. Whenever I hear you speak about marriage relationships, I become more aware of how I must really feel about my wife. Your periodic talks about people's marriages actually hurt mine. You know why? Because you uncovered bad aspects of our marriage. I think I started to learn to live with a 'blah' marriage, until you came along with your talks and began to point out how bad things really were."

Does my breakfast partner see me unconsciously squirm

under this observation? Now *I* feel uneasy! *He's right,* I think to myself. *A lot of people learn to live with various kinds of relational pain, until it really ceases to be pain. It simply becomes part of their overall feeling, a kind of numbness. Content with weakness and mediocrity, they accept a fourth-class life-style. Then someone like myself reminds them of what could or should be, and the old pain comes on again.*

Instinctively I want to protest, to explain myself. But I decide to listen, and when I mentally return to the conversation, I hear him saying, ". . . At least I don't feel about my wife the way *you say* husbands should." Again I want to correct his language, to tell him that it's not what *I say,* but what the Bible says. He doesn't give me time. He says once again, "Do you think you understand what I'm trying to say?" When I nod yes, he continues.

"We've got a good marriage, I guess. At least I've never been unfaithful. We don't argue either, no serious fights anyway. In fact, if you asked me to tell you what's wrong with our marriage, I'm not sure I could tell you."

It's obvious that the further my friend goes, the harder it becomes to assign words to the things he feels and experiences. But entered into the discussion too deeply to stop talking now, he takes a quick sip of the coffee and goes back for another start at describing his life. I sip, too, reminding myself that he's probably planned this conversation for a long time and that it has taken his every ounce of nerve to speak this candidly.

"I'm trying to say that my marriage is flat—just like my job. I don't care what time it is when I get home in the evening. For example, you said that husbands are supposed to feel excited about getting home. I don't! I guess I know that it's always going to be the same when I get there. I *know* she's going to cook a decent meal, that clean socks will sit in the drawer, that I can have sex just about any time I want. And that's what confuses me. Why isn't there some sort of excitement? Why, with half of my life left, has everything seemed to have lost its color? Think of it: a good job, a good wife—but nothing in the way of feelings about either of them. I should feel more thankful, but I don't. You'd think I lived in a pool of Novocain: nothing.

"Do you know what I think about doing sometimes?" he asks. In response to the curiosity question marked on my face, he says, "I'd like to kiss the job and the wife good-bye and just disappear into some whole new way of life. I'd like to walk away from everything, start all over again, become a new person. I find myself thinking about that possibility all the time." Then he again reveals his anxiety about the impression all of this may be having upon me when he says again, "I hope this all doesn't shock you too much."

I'm not shocked; I'm not surprised. I've listened to his kind of story before—different versions, same themes. In fact, if any uniqueness exists in what he says, it is in the fact that he's said it at all. Because most men, as I tell him, would have kept these feelings bottled up within them. They would not have suggested a breakfast date with a pastor or a friend and would not have explained to anyone the current status of their morale. A quiet, subsurface undertow of thought might one day explode without warning, with terrible consequences for everyone in the immediate vicinity. So I affirm the man across the table for opening his life up to someone, and I suggest that the very fact that he can describe his feelings is a positive clue to the relative health of his situation.

"What you're saying quite plainly," I continue, "is that you don't think yourself to be a very happy man at this point in your life."

"No, I'm not happy. I enjoy some good times, but to describe myself as a happy man . . . ? No! I couldn't do that! It's strange that I would answer you in that way. I thought unhappy people experienced things gone wrong in their lives. I can't think of many things that have gone wrong in *my* life. No sickness, no financial reverses. A few big bills, probably. But nothing I couldn't work my way out of. The kids haven't given trouble. At least the job has been steady. But I don't feel happy."

He's thinking out loud now, sharing snap thoughts as they pour through his mind. "I guess I did think at one time that I'd be higher in the company by now. But that was before I really knew what it took to get to the top."

He pauses again, stares at the wall, talks again, "That's funny; I have no reason to be unhappy. Nothing bad has happened. But *I'm not a happy man.* Does being 'not happy' mean that you are unhappy?"

We go on to talk about his family, elements of his life as husband and father. No, he's not close to his son. And yes he wishes he were. He has no particular hobby; he doesn't really ever look forward to anything. He has many friends, but no close ones. The use of most evenings? Watching television.

Then I ask about God, and he confirms what I suspect. His relationship to God is, by his definition, distant and ineffectual. I am bothered by that. My friend has grown up in the church for thirty-nine years. After all that time, God remains an apparent enigma to him.

"I was afraid you'd ask me that question," he says. More coffee. "My religious life is a loser. I've never had that part of me together. Look: no great sins, okay? I've just never been able to take prayer and Bible reading seriously. Every once in a while, our family has a devotional time because you or someone else encourages it, but we forget it pretty soon. Everyone's too busy."

Disappointment in vocation, disappointment in relationships, now disappointment in the circle of his beliefs. He called his life "flat." What should he do? I suspect that when we leave the coffee shop in another twenty minutes, my friend with the "flat" life will add one more disappointment to his life: disappointment in me.

He's come looking for some kind of monumental insight or answer to his problem. That's why most people initially approach a pastor or a counselor. They hope to turn up the loose "thread," which when tucked back in, will make everything suddenly turn out all right. I think my friend suspects I own some secret about living. And if I confide it to him, he'll be able to make everything come out in his life.

But when he leaves the restaurant, he may conclude that either I'm not smart enough to have the secret or, assuming that I am smart enough, that I'm not going to loan it out to him. He may suspect I've let him down when I tell him that the answer to his struggles rests in taking time for reversing destructive patterns of living. My listing of certain mental and spiritual disciplines he probably ought to employ and a few patterns he ought to avoid seems too practical and unspectacular in terms of an obvious solution. He hoped to acquire quick and easy answers. If he does think such thoughts, will he come back and talk with me again? I worry about that.

If he proposes another conversation, I shall begin to talk about the phenomenon of high noon, because he is there. But I shall try to point out to him first of all that his problems and struggles are not *caused* by this stage of life; rather they are *exposed* by it.

Something very simple happened. The "flatness" of his relationships and vocation has been in process for some time. In younger years, he could excuse actions and apathies by simply suggesting to himself that things would be better "someday."

I sense that my friend has fallen into a fatal circuit of thinking. For example, when he faced rough moments in his career five to eight years ago, perhaps he reasoned that more experience and a consolidation of departmental power through a promotion would wash away his problems. Or when confronted with the evidence of an increasingly insipid marital relationship at home, he probably turned from the facts and reasoned that, given a little time, "things would blow over."

His high-noon experience begins to show that things ignored or put off into the indefinite future do not blow over, nor do they generally wash away. Now the consequences of earlier choices made or avoided show themselves. He doesn't like it.

He uneasily feels the walls closing around him, that things appear to be moving beyond the extent of his control. Professionally he worries about security and success; relationally he worries about boredom and isolation; spiritually he discovers himself dry and bereft of resources.

A second thing I'll try to show him in our next conversation is that his problems are not unique. To a greater or lesser extent, he joins many men and women who have suddenly awakened one morning to find that everything important has become colorless. These high-noon people enter mid-life, where matters of living tend to lose the gloss of high hopes and strong enthusiasm. But this need not happen. Call it high noon, call it mid-life, but don't call it irrevocably colorless, as so many have. The high-noon dramas may be universal, but they can also be filled with excitement.

I will try to help him to see that his present bewilderment will probably turn to bitterness if not treated. In the end, he could start to blame the cause of his feelings upon others: his boss, his wife, his parents, and probably his church. If he continues to feel powerless today, he will feel defeated tomorrow. If he continues to feel flat today, he will feel flattened tomorrow. And without some sort of corrective brought to bear, he will either run from the dramas (escapism) or he will cave in to a long, slow, spiritual and mental decay (capitulation).

If our next conversation continues, I'll try to point out a third aspect of his struggle. I'll attempt to show him how he can discover the roots of his present feelings and consequences. Somehow, he'll have to look back over thirty-nine years of life and see where he made critical choices and absorbed essential styles of living that brought him to this moment. He will have to evaluate these facts in his heart and mind and see his right and wrong choices. Hopefully, he'll come to a point where he assumes the responsibility for today's life. If he can do that, he can probably begin to make broad, sweeping changes in his mid-life, which will relieve the present painful situation.

Then I will find it relatively easy to help him work through the alterations of relationships and attitudes to the significant things in his life: God, his wife, his growing children, his friends. But without such changes, he will walk into the afternoon and evening of his life with regret and recrimination.

As I watch him unlock his car and swing it into the morning traffic, I think once again about the tragedy he has woven about himself. I can't help but brood about this hurting man, and the cause of his ache is rooted in choices made that now become clearer and clearer in terms of their consequences. When he drives off, I turn and walk toward the battlegreen and once again become aware of the half-mast flag. Symbolically, it hangs there for my befuddled friend.

Out of affection for him, I silently vow to walk with him until the day that the "flag" of his life returns to its proper place: the top. And because I feel optimistic and positive about the potential results of the high-noon dramas, I'll stick with him all the way.

3
The Bad Press of Middle Age

When one of my neighbors heard of my fascination with the high-noon dramas and of my intention to write about them, she offered a number of unsolicited comments. Our conversation covered depression, psychic pain, and personality change, but I most remember her conclusion about the whole matter of middle age: "Middle age is the cruelest joke in life so far. If I had known what was coming, I'd either have stayed thirty-five or made a big jump to fifty-five. Either age is better than this."

In a day of political minority groups, I suspect she would have been a prime candidate for membership in a "Mid-life Liberation Front." She simply voices another version of many negative conversations I've had about middle age, in which the mid-lifer employs a depressing vocabulary. She actually feels oppressed. Things are happening to her; she resents them and talks in bitter terms. My mind snaps to the question asked at my breakfast meeting, "What's happening to me?" These two people think that life is spinning out of control.

In public-relations language, they are giving middle age bad press. They use descriptive words like *betrayed,* if they talk about punctured dreams; *trapped,* if they brood upon things they can't escape; *obsolete,* if they reflect on how quickly the world changes about them; and *passed by,* if they admit their career goals lie shattered in pieces. Alternative words might include *bored, hassled, tired* and *panicky.*

In these conversations the fact that descriptions of mid-life are all too often negative impresses me. Why does mid-life receive such bad press? Why are those within this age frame frequently defensive in much the way of one person in our church, who said rather candidly to me, "Call us middle adults, not middle-aged." Do even the word choices bother some of us? A woman says of her husband, "The day he hit his fortieth birthday, he went into some kind of mild depression; he hasn't been the same for six months now." Does the celebration of one more birthday actually have that kind of impact upon some people? Why?

Having listened, watched, studied, and mixed it with a modest amount of experience, I discover several reasons for the almost universal instinctive fear of mid-life among peoples of Western cultures.

Mark down as a key possibility the matter of *ignorance and unpreparedness.* Beyond the students of adult development, only those in transit through these years seem to know anything about middle life. But they themselves remained ignorant about the mid-life issues, to an extent, until they arrived there. Not knowing what to expect, their life-style tends to be one of *reaction* to the events of middle life rather than one of *initiation.* That I suppose forms an essential pivotal point at which one decides for himself whether or not the mid-life experience is to be positive or negative.

I first became interested in the high-noon period of life because I saw so many unprepared people facing such situations and stresses. I offered an evening seminar on the middle years, and fifty people signed up. Without exception, these men and women had already well advanced into the mid-life period. For six weeks we met each Tuesday evening. I brought together the materials I discovered at libraries and other resource centers, and we oohed and aahed our way through fascinating descriptions and analyses of what we all faced. Frequent laughter rang out as people found that they alone did not face certain fears or struggles. During moments of intense thought, we discussed the sources or explanations for present experiences. Not a week passed that many did not say in or after the sessions, "If only someone had forced us to face these things fifteen years ago, *we could have been ready.* We would have saved ourselves so much frustration."

"We could have been ready. . . ." Most people are not ready for any stage of advancing life. Few couples are ready for marriage; few are ready for parenthood; very few are ready for mid-life. And even fewer prepare for the years of defined retirement. The result? They spend up to 25 percent of the period of an adult stage floundering, struggling to find the handles that assist in bringing the issues of that period under control.

Readiness depends upon the availability of information and the willingness of people to use it to their best advantage. The quantity of information on the middle years grows larger and larger every year, but whether or not people willingly use the data remains to be seen.

Most of us automatically react, "It can't happen to us." Accidents, tragedies, bankruptcies, we reason, all happen to "others." We extend this fantasy to the concept of middle life. But it happens to us! And if we have denied its inexorable movement toward us during our younger years, we may not be ready to live with it upon its arrival.

Perhaps one of the reasons we tend to be ignorant and unready for the succession of stages in life centers on our Western culture's tendency to segment society by age groupings. As a people we may have lost the extended-family concept in which grandparents, uncles, and aunts share the same basic family experience with younger parents and children. In days past there existed an intergenerational support group that brought each person to an awareness of each stage of life. The old system provided the resources of comfort, advice, and assistance whenever any particular individual faced a crisis or challenge. Today our mobile culture has broken up the extended family to such an extent that each age group now remains on its own, responsible for itself. Stripped of the support and insight of the previous generation, one stands on new ground, with little guidance to make the journey.

Try this relatively simple solution: *Prepare* five years ahead for each new stage. One ought to be a student of the middle years by the time he or she is thirty-two and be in preparation for retirement by the mid-forties. Carl Jung said things like that four decades ago, but while everyone may have found it easy to agree, no one found it easy to implement the proposals.

The people who wish they'd been in the seminar on mid-life fifteen years earlier indicate the need for preparation when they wistfully say, "If only someone had told us. . . ." But they could not answer with certainty when I asked if they thought they would really have been interested in studying a future stage of life.

When it comes to an analysis of why mid-life engenders so much bad press, ignorance of the experience ranks at the top of explanations. But we may need to go deeper for an even more extensive view. I'd like to suggest that much aversion to the high-noon experience centers upon a package of three facts of living. The three come in three dimensions. First, note that mid-life normally presents a person with his or her first major evaluation of the past, of how productive life has been. Second, mid-life confronts one with a series of unique, previously un-experienced stresses. Finally, mid-life raises the first obvious warning flags about death.

I wish I could skip the first of those three ideas. But I can't! Mid-life brings us to the first significant subtotaling experience of life. A good adding machine has a subtotal button on it, and when the user punches that button, he gets an idea of the progress made so far.

For the first time in our lives, certain events confront us that give us no choice but to make a subtotaling of our efforts. Take our children, for example. They have reached the age of semi-independent performance, usually the mid-adolescent period, the verge of adulthood. We see them as products of the environment we have created in our homes. They now make their own choices, standing on their own convictions, whatever those may be. We no longer enjoy effective control over their personalities and values. The result may seem painful or delightful; but they have become what they will be.

Football fans will tell you that, early in the season, many coaches send the choices of plays into the huddle through players who rotate in and out of the game. The quarterback gets the play from them and executes it. But later in the season, the coach may choose to allow the quarterback to make his own choices. What's happened? He has released the team to perform according to previous training and experience. The scores tell how well this has worked. If their success is a credit to the coach, their failure unmasks him as an ineffective leader.

I'd like to suggest that the mid-life parent no longer sends in plays for his children to carry out. He now stands on the sidelines, forced to face the fruits of his parenting. Like the coach, he or she cannot run to the locker room, out of embarrassment, if the score begins to turn sour. Many people self-consciously and subconsciously fear and wish to avoid that painful vulnerability. But that's part of mid-life. The subtotal button has been punched.

The same kind of subtotaling often happens, as we shall later see in some detail, in the vocational aspect of our lives. We begin to face the unavoidable answer to the question, Have we really achieved what we considered to be success? Everyone measures success differently. Some see it in terms of position, some in terms of income, others in terms of recognition, still others in terms of new opportunities. Whatever our chosen criteria for success or failure, the subtotal answer tends to come in the mid-life experience.

Perhaps the difficulty results from our putting off evaluation during earlier years. We employ various kinds of rationales that postpone evaluation.

In our earliest years we could say, "When I grow up, I'll do that more thoroughly or more neatly or more productively." In our young adult years, we reason, "When I gain more experience, I'll produce more widgets, greater volumes of sales, better quality decisions." And in our pre-mid-life period, we argue, "When I'm recognized or get the chance, I'll show them what I've got to offer."

The avoidance process reminds me of a young student who resists the truth about grades through one examination after another, promising that the next time things will improve. But one day there comes a report card with bad news. Anyone in that condition learns to despise report cards. It dawns on me that the only people who slept well the night before report cards and actually welcomed their distribution were the ones who had consistently worked hard at every point of the semester and who had not kept making excuses for themselves. I suspect that is true about both the report card and subtotaling experience of mid-life.

Mid-life tells on us; it reveals what our family is actually like, whether or not we've taken care of our bodies, if we became all we thought we could be vocationally, and it tends to expose the depth of our commitment to certain spiritual truths. No wonder a lot of people bad-mouth mid-life. Those suffering from a lack of self-confidence might like to avoid that kind of subtotaling.

The man I met for breakfast at the Pewter Pot admits with his tongue slightly in cheek that he doesn't like to listen to his pastor talk about marriage. Why? Because talking about marriage draws a straight line against the crooked one of his relationship with his wife. Rather than assuming the perspective that the measurement will show him where to make changes, he feels tempted to turn away from the straight line, because *he has grown used to the crooked one.* In effect he says, "I don't want anyone telling or showing me that I've made some bad choices. It's too unsettling and revealing."

If people do not wish to look backwards, they don't often welcome the present-tense experience that mid-life purports to offer either. And that's another reason why one hears little cheering about being middle-aged. Reports of certain events and personal experiences at mid-life that seem anything but attractive bombard us: female menopause, male impotence, infidelity, depression, hot or cold flashes, incessant irritability, weight gain, heart attacks—ugh! The list seems to drag on until I even get depressed writing down the things I hear about. Let's face it, with a list like that (if it is accurate) one might be forced to agree with my neighbor: Mid-life is a cruel joke; let's vote it out of existence.

To some extent we return to the subject of ignorance—ignorance about what these reports really mean. For example, we might not unreasonably suggest that those complaining of some elements of this long list of psychic, emotional, and physical maladies number few compared to those who have not experienced these kinds of distresses. It just so happens that—as the old law of human nature dictates—the hurting cry louder than the nonhurting.

Much of the intense opposition to middle life often flows out of a superficial interpretation of the most valuable and significant matters of existence. If a woman has traded for twenty years on the currency of her natural beauty as her purchasing power for acceptance by her peers, mid-life comes as a painful shock. The laws of physiology create changes of shape and form that will erode youthful attractiveness. Not that she ceases to be physically charming; but the basis of that beauty will tie much more directly to personality and character traits, something not necessarily true in the earlier adult years. There is little—short of the allocation of large sums of money, and that only for a brief time—that such a troubled person can do about such a change. The onset of such shifts and no viable alternatives for acceptance and popularity make mid-life unacceptable.

I have seen the same pattern in the experience of a man who enjoyed early success in life not through hard work and self-discipline but rather through the sheer charisma and natural talent with which youth is sometimes blessed. But years pass, and before one is aware, the energies, the cleverness, and the abilities that came easily cannot keep pace with the rising need for wisdom, discretion, and self-control. Something half in the conscious and perhaps half in the subconscious causes one to be aware that mid-life will expose deficiencies in character and stamina in the push for the top in life's achievements. What I'm trying to point out in both cases—the woman with fading natural beauty and the man with dissipating energy—is that these kinds of people facing new and disquieting stresses have few complimentary words about life in the middle years.

I believe the strange fear of the mid-life segment often results from the temptation to think of its traumas as *terminal* rather than *transitional.* A man fears the termination of his sexual experience either because his wife enters menopause or because he himself might face impotence. He thinks terminally. Should he begin to think transitionally, he may discover, to his relief and delight, his sexual experience enhanced and improved at mid-life as he and his wife gain more privacy, flexibility of schedule, greater knowledge of each other's needs and desires, not to speak of the lack of fear of an undesired pregnancy.

A person may think mid-life exposes his limits and liabilities in vocation. He sees mid-life as a time of leveling off, of becoming a "nobody," a person passed by better or younger competitors. But that same man might adopt a transitional perspective that proposes that a limit revealed in one area of life might actually point to an opportunity in another area. For the first time in life, he discovers alternatives that far exceed original ambitions. Transitional thinking releases the one-track mind that sees mid-life only in terms of failure or success. It discloses whole new vistas of activity that, given a more mature mind, far outstrip the choices of earlier days.

For several days I stay in the home of a middle-aged couple who reside in a foreign country. They apparently live in a total enjoyment of each day, relaxed, discovering new things about their world, and—most important—having a direct and measurable opportunity to serve God as they procure supplies and provide communications for a missionary team spread hundreds of miles across rural and jungle lands. When I visit with them about their odyssey in life, I discover that it begins with the husband's brutal experience of failure in an earlier vocation. With some associates, he'd started a business that temporarily succeeded and then collapsed in bankruptcy. He smiles ruefully as he talks about how each of the men on that business team faced that failure. One began to drink heavily; another sank into depression; the others, determined to succeed, decided to try again. But the man who relates the story to me saw this as a time to ask questions of a transitional character. A personal failure in this case became a release into something far more exciting and rewarding. A lot less money, not much notoriety, but more satisfaction, he says, than anyone deserves in a lifetime. I put him down as a transitional thinker. Present realities do not intimidate him.

An old Alka-Seltzer slogan once read, "Perhaps the circumstances won't change; but you can!" There is the answer to those who wrestle with the present-tense realities of mid-life. While the circumstances of change are inevitable, the choice to face them from a terminal or transitional perspective belongs to the person and what he or she chooses makes all the difference.

If I ventured one more possible explanation for the poor public-relations image of the middle years, it would have to center on the future—the impending fact of death. People do die; everything living dies sooner or later. But apart from some unexpected tragedy, most of us generally avoid the facts of death for almost forty years of living. Modern hospitals and medical techniques protect the majority of us from ever seeing a person die. It was not always that way.

My mother recalls the 1930 deathbed scene of her father. An entire family sat for hours, not in a hospital lounge but in the front bedroom at home while Grandfather Nordquist sank deeper and deeper into the weakness of approaching death. A few final words to each family member, the singing of a Christian hymn, and he bowed his head and died. This was not an unusual experience for families for many centuries, but we rarely see it today. Then, death played a part in life; today it does not. Death, in fact, almost always borders on being the ultimate obscenity. One writer called it "the great American unspeakable." If someone does in fact die, we surround the death with an incredible air of unreality. Expensive flowers, funerals, vast corteges of people and limousines, magnificent cemeteries that try to gloss over the unmitigated bare facts that death has its time.

Covering up death makes it all the more mysterious. We fear it because we do not understand it and because we remain unprepared for it. At mid-life we slowly confront its movement toward us.

I cannot provide the reasons, but many men tell me of a time of inner depression in their mid-thirties as they first become aware of the all-encompassing reality of death. For the first time the fact strikes them that someday (they are not sure which one) they will personally experience death: theirs. It seems so final. Ambitions, plans, energies, relationships will be turned off. They can do nothing to control it. They must simply wait for it to initiate the encounter.

That lack of control is probably what bothers negative-thinking people most of all about mid-life. They think they sense an approaching conglomerate of situations where more and more things will seem out of control. And death becomes the final out-of-control reality. Bodies change, out of control. Children make their decisions, and a parent feels out of control. Friends change in terms of their personalities, and it feels as if relationships zoom out of control. Does all of life suddenly seem out of control for the mid-lifer?

A close friend of mine recently visited the National Gallery of Art, in Washington, D.C. While there, he became fascinated with the artistry of a nineteenth-century painter, Thomas Cole. Cole's greatest works include a series of four paintings entitled "The Voyages of Life." The first of the series, called *Childhood,* depicts a boat emerging from darkness, with a beautiful child looking breathlessly at all the new sights about him. At the stern of the boat an angel stands as guardian, with a firm hand on the rudder, guiding the boat with the child in the proper direction.

The second painting is called *Youth.* Some things have changed now. The angel stands on shore; the child, now a young adult, has the rudder in his own hand. As the angel waves good-bye, the youth—obviously unmindful of the heavenly guardian—looks off to the horizon, waving at it with obvious dreams of conquest and possession. The sky in front of the boat is lit with the faint illusions of a magnificent castle, symbolizing power and success.

But 125 years ago Thomas Cole also perceived another phase of life, and he called it the third of the series *Manhood.* We'd call it middle life. In this third painting the once bright horizon appears dark, while a vicious storm approaches the boat. The once tranquil waters form a raging torrent, with rapids, rocks, and overhanging trees ready to rip at anything near them. In the boat, the voyager no longer stands confidently at the helm with the rudder. With the rudder broken, the boat careers out of control. The confident young man seems ridden with fear, and he kneels, raising folded hands toward heaven.

I sit and brood upon Cole's depiction of manhood. How did he know our plight so well? How could he have seen the dilemma of modern men and women, who face mid-life and perceive it as a section of life out of control? For them aging becomes a death process, and they cannot impede the speed of that process or modify its mysterious conclusion.

Cole has painted what I try to write. In mid-life modern persons detect the reality of death. They sense decay in their physiological change and limitations. They smell mortality in the relational modifications happening about them. They think they see the end in the diminishing prospects for predefined success. They experience the touch of death when they feel so far from God. Thus the process only serves to point the way to their actual demise. And that does not look like a bright prospect.

Saint Paul lived with death. He'd seen people die; he'd been left for dead several times. The death of Jesus Christ, whom he preached, was a cardinal point of doctrine in his teaching. Thus this matter was no stranger to him. Perhaps for that reason he never seems to have feared it. When he wrote to the Christian church at Philippi, he said:

> For to me, living means opportunities for Christ, and dying—well, that's better yet! But if living will give me more opportunities to win people to Christ, then I really don't know which is better, to live or die! Sometimes I want to live and at other times I don't, for I long to go and be with Christ. . . . But the fact is that I can be of more help to *you* by staying!
>
> Philippians 1:21–24 TLB

Paul shares his incredible view of death and life with us. Obviously neither the process nor the point of death intimidates him, for at least two reasons. First, Paul sees life in terms of serving in the world around him. To him, life means giving and therefore growing.

In contrast, the people who fear the process and the point of death seem *self-oriented* rather than *other oriented.* The gaining of things, the pursuit of power, the amassing of recognition mean that one has a lot to lose through death. Thus reminders of it can be rather distressing. Saint Paul never lived under that kind of crippling obsession. Death couldn't take away anything really important to him. Thus it ceased to be his enemy. The result? No depression, no avoidance techniques, no self-pity.

Second, Paul teaches us that death is not terminal but transitional. The Christian, by his faith, affirms an eternal life experience that, as Paul puts it, means to be with Christ. For Paul that meant a new and improved body, an enlarged mind, and an unlimited opportunity to pursue things he had been made for. So should he face execution at the behest of Nero, the pagan Roman emperor, it would be a gateway experience to heaven.

I don't think Paul for one moment relished the moment of dying. Who would? But he became committed to the bigger picture, and in that setting, he viewed death as not even a minor irritant to life.

In another place, Paul suggested that he died a little bit daily. Was Paul facing the death process, in effect? I think so. He accepted change, transition. He welcomed the opportunities it presents. Thus, no fear, no weakness, no loss of confidence.

You would never have gotten Paul to bad-mouth mid-life. First of all, he wouldn't have had time. The discovery of how much he could do with every available hour kept him too busy. To Paul aging did not mean growing older, but rather growing more mature, becoming one step closer to total living with Christ.

Henri Nouwen gives some insight into the stamina produced by transitional thinking when he describes a confrontation in a World War II German concentration camp between a Lutheran bishop and an SS officer seeking a confession politically advantageous to the Nazis. The refusal of the bishop to comply with his inquisitor's wishes brought torture. But the pain could not break the determined will of the prisoner. Thus he stood silently while the officer grew more and more outraged. He received more and more blows, harder and harder, until the German finally shouted to the bishop, "Don't you know that I can kill you?"

Storyteller Nouwen describes the look the bishop gave as he said slowly, "Yes, I know—do what you want—but I have already died." The interrogation ended! The officer's power was broken, and his seemingly paralyzed arm told a story in physical terms. No leverage weighs against a person with no fear of death. All the blows one could muster against him would be empty and futile.

Mid-lifers should ponder this. Transitional thinking dissolves those roots of past, present, and future fear that in turn activate moods like dread and depression. If life's circumstances include any moments of torture, the man or woman with transitional thinking styles sees the bigger picture—where all of this is heading. You won't get any bad opinions about middle age from such people.

My neighbor—the one who speaks of cruel jokes—thinks terminally. Thus, she smiles when I try to point out the marvelous opportunities that could flow from the dramas of high noon. She's not convinced, and neither are many other middle adults who never prepared ahead of time for that period of life when a transitional perspective makes sense out of it all.

4
Taking a Trip to Denver

It bothers me that I can't convince my neighbor that some good pieces of news come along with mid-life. As I think over our sidewalk conversation a parable occurs to me. It springs from an experience in my past. See if it speaks to the point: that mid-life is either good news or bad news, depending upon one's attitude and response to unavoidable circumstances.

Perhaps I could begin by saying that if you ever choose to drive westward from Saint Francis, Kansas, to Denver, Colorado, I can tell you everything you'll need to know about the trip. Among the trivia I have stored in my mental data bank come the facts that the distance between Saint Francis and Denver is 176 miles; there are twelve significant curves, the rest of the two-lane road being arrow straight; and eight prairie towns dot the way, none of which are open for business after six in the evening or before seven in the morning.

I know all that, and much more, because I once drove back and forth on U.S. Route 36 between a little rural church of a dozen delightful farming families and a seminary in the large city of Denver. Twice each week I left our country parsonage at 4:00 A.M. and arrived on campus just in time for a 7:30 A.M. class in theology. A gas-thrifty Volkswagen Beetle (usually driven most of the way in third gear, instead of fourth, because of prevailing headwinds) provided transportation.

For the first two-thirds of my twice-weekly journey, the western horizon remained clear. The Colorado Plains are pancake flat, and (this is important) I sometimes used to nurse the illusion that I could turn the VW in any direction, launch out across the prairie, and drive forever, with or without the benefit of a road. It seemed as if nothing would have hindered me, except of course an empty gas tank.

But all good illusions come to an end, and mine always dissipated just after I passed through the town of Last Chance, Colorado (actually a place with a United States post office). At the top of a slight rise in the road I could suddenly see the distant tips of Pikes Peak to the south and Longs Peak to the north, each a bit higher than 14,000 feet in altitude. The vestiges of my illusion of unhindered westward travel slowly dissolved within the next twenty miles down U.S. Route 36 as other lesser Rocky Mountain peaks hove into view one at a time until a jagged wall of snow-capped mountains filled the entire landscape before me.

By the time I reached the limits of Denver at 7:00 A.M. the Rocky Mountains, just west of the city, *appeared* as a formidable barrier to any further forward travel. Denver seemed the end of the world, and one could go no farther. In the space of a hundred miles an illusion shifted full circle. Originally no barriers to one's travel arose on the horizon. But now at the edge of Denver an obstacle blocked the way. Once no barriers; now no passage.

Obviously, both impressions (once no barrier; now no passage) are false. But at the point in time when one visualizes them, they profoundly exhilarate the imagination on the one hand and terribly intimidate one's spirit on the other. The first message read: You *can* go anywhere. The second: You *can't* go anywhere.

Of course the mountains restrict one's options in terms of direction of travel; still holes exist through the mountains, canyons, passes, even tunnels. But as long as the surprised and shocked traveler stands at the city limits of Denver and refuses to go further westward, he won't locate them.

Consider the series of thoughts in my description of a trip to Denver. Hopefully the parable provides insight on the actions and attitudes many men and women in the aging process exhibit as they near that period of living called mid-life. All of us—including my discouraged neighbor—travel to Denver and beyond. The closer we come to this Rocky Mountain wall, the more we learn about ourselves and the more we face certain choices about how we'll perform when we get there. Think through some of the options with me.

In the early phases of a symbolic trip to Denver—our young adulthood—there seem to be no limits, no barriers within our expectancies of what life will present to us. In the illusory state of enthusiasm, we perceive that any direction and any speed seem reasonably possible. A friend of mine muses upon my parable of travel, agrees with the imagery of speeding across the eastern plains, and reflects nostalgically, "When I was twenty-one, I was quietly convinced that I could do anything—even be president of the United States, if I wanted the position bad enough. With the right breaks, I thought the sky was the limit."

I think he speaks for a lot of us. In our younger years, energy seems unlimited; our faith in our personal capacities usually remains unbounded. I can hear someone wanting to remind me that significant numbers of people prove the exceptions to this generalization. Brought up in an economically disadvantaged context, they have never viewed anything but a life of unobstructed horizons. In fact, their eyes may stay instinctively glued on the ground beneath their feet (the momentary, the present) for fear that circumstances could snatch even that out from under them. We might also have to concede this exception for those who for various reasons never achieved an experience of self-acceptance or worth because of poisoned family or peer relationships. In truth, they may stand on the city limits of Denver, looking morosely at the mountains, with their jagged obstacles, sooner than anyone else. Nevertheless, I would argue that generally youth contains a heavy overdose of enthusiasm and expectancy.

Our personal trips to Denver, no matter how swift, are a process of change and scenery. And with that process comes the appearance of the first jagged peaks—finger sized at first, but nevertheless disturbing hints of "unknowns" that could spell potential trouble. One may not at first consider them as limiting factors in life. But think for a moment about the growing implications of the birth of a baby, necessary financial obligations, patterns of recurring illness, jobs with hazy opportunities for advancement or meaningful achievement. Stir in the mistakes and the miscalculations made in the normal course of living. Each represents a new kind of mountain peak on the horizon.

The inevitable result? A horizon of once unlimited opportunity becomes swiftly cluttered with more and more "obstacles," until one long, seemingly impenetrable wall rises before us. Optimism gives way to uneasiness, sometimes even quiet fear or inner panic. That's why when one reaches "Denver," the onset of mid-life, the illusion seems to have fully shifted to something that whispers that the last part of a trip may be over. We see nothing to look forward to anymore. Something has gone sour.

My neighbor, the one who thinks of middle age as a cruel joke, stands at the edge of Denver and thinks her trip has turned into a "bummer." The mountains apparently signal the end of forward progress.

The men and women who arrive at "Denver's" city limits size up the mountains just ahead, experiencing several general reactions. We'll note them briefly and evaluate the healthiest reactions.

One standard response from among those reaching "Denver" is to want to turn around and attempt to return to the east—the good old days when the horizons appeared more promising. Historically, by the way, many discouraged pioneers did just that. They saw nothing good about Denver and the land just beyond it, so they turned around and went back home.

If that mountainous wall represents the dramas of mid-life, let me point out that more than a few persons in our culture actually experiment with a frantic "turnaround," fleeing back to the place of youth. I will want to come back to this common response in its various forms in several subsequent chapters. A flight backward to youth: frequently seen in a mid-lifer's choice of college-style clothing, hairstyles, entertainment, and even in romantic relationships with younger men or women.

I watch a lot of people trying to run away from the wall. I'm tempted to try it myself on occasion. One group turns their backs on it, trying to pretend that it never existed. In a church setting, for example, the strenuous resistance one puts up in moving to an older age-group Sunday-school class or a fellowship group may hint at dissatisfaction with mid-life. For the resisters, a temporary prolonging of the myth of youthfulness might result, but the ultimate consequence of not accepting the trip to Denver turns to a biting bitterness when the myth ultimately explodes—usually in embarrassment or humiliation.

A once vibrant and beautiful movie star, now seventy, says after five or six face-lifts, many younger lovers, and a vain attempt to lie about her age, "Do you think for one moment that life is worth a ... thing when you're old?" She's one of a select few who through the use of unlimited amounts of money and the "freedoms" frequently afforded by our society to artists and models, has been able to put off the aging process, at least in terms of image. She kept running away from the aging process for a long time, but now the fight ends. Her overnight jump from thirty-nine to seventy seems brutal. No wonder she responds in anger. As I'll try to show in future chapters, people try a variety of ways to return eastward. They never succeed, but they keep on trying.

A second group of folk on the trip to Denver reach the mountains but possess neither the courage to push ahead nor the nerve to go back. So they just camp there, perhaps traveling in gigantic circles—covering ground, but really going nowhere. They look wistfully backward to the past and fearfully forward to the future, but they settle down for a while, going "no-ward."

I think I'm sketching the mid-life quitter, one of a large group of persons we meet every day, who appears to have lost momentum in the pursuit of living. He has released his hold on the initiative, relinquished many previous objectives and goals, and begun simply to let things happen to him. It becomes a passive way of living.

Want a few symptoms of those who "camp" near the wall? Bodies are permitted to grow flabby; ambition to make a difference in the world atrophies; marriages grow insipid, even boring. Careers degenerate into tiring jobs; faith becomes routine; cynicism and disbelief mark attitudes. The overarching mentality becomes one of self-preservation, limited commitment, and the avoidance of risk, vulnerability, or generosity.

That's Archie Bunker, a sad mid-lifer whose world has degenerated into his guaranteeing the sanctity of his easy chair, asserting his right to a cold beer when he gets home, and maintaining a frantic protection of values and attitudes that he attributes to his good old days. Archie pictures an extreme extension of the kind of person who arrives at Denver but fears pressing on ahead.

I've said all this because I wanted to draw the contrasts that make the third group of people on the trip to Denver so exciting. These travelers determinedly surge on ahead, believing that in "them thar hills" lies unlimited opportunity for discovery and achievement. These mid-life people are not fooled by bare horizons or seemingly impenetrable walls.

Let me describe these people to you. On the trip westward, long before reaching Last Chance (remember the small town I previously mentioned), they studied life's map. They learned several things and came prepared. They understand the implications of proverbs such as "A sensible man watches for problems ahead and prepares to meet them. The simpleton never looks, and suffers the consequences" (Proverbs 27:12 TLB). Along with that, they relax with another proverb that reminds

them "Since the Lord is directing our steps, why try to understand everything that happens along the way?" (Proverbs 20:24
TLB). For example they know that Denver is by no means the
terminus point for westward travelers. Every stage of the trip
presents unique challenges, they realize, and for them challenges spell opportunity for growth, not disaster. After all, the
proverbs indicated that, didn't they?

The kind of person I'm describing anticipates the discovery
of "holes" in the wall—the valleys, passes, and tunnels that
will provide a way through. They'll take the "wall" by storm.
Living in the mountains will mean a new experience—the best
part of the trip so far.

What overriding mark of character does one see in this type
of person? I'd call it *confidence*. A brand of authentic (not artificial) confidence grounded in the conviction that the God of
all life also remains the God of mid-life. Such a person views
the dramas of high noon neither as accidents nor a phase of
aging that shows up a colossal error on God's part. This confidence suggests that one may experience in mid-life something
not found at any other time of one's existence.

The confident middle-ager of whom I speak is not a common species of human being. I suspect that the reason lies in
the fact that few persons attempt to describe some of the mid-
life possibilities. That's probably my neighbor's problem as she
bitterly circles at the Denver city limits. She majors on all the
problems; she needs to muse upon the possibilities. If she'd
permit further discussion on the topic, I'd probably list several
possibilities that offer potential good feelings about the trip
through the mountains.

I'd propose, for example, that mid-life may, for the first time,
provide the potential of an interruption in the unceasing
pressures of young adulthood. Yes, pressures! Before anyone
gets overexcited about returning to youth, could we remind
ourselves that youth, with all of its excitement, also entails incredible pressures? I am not much impressed with the accumulating stream of tension and stress produced by the founding

and developing of some sort of career, the establishment of a marriage, the first twelve to fifteen years of child raising, and the struggle to find out who one actually is as he or she springs out from under peer pressure and away from parental authority.

On a midwestern trip I sit at a family dinner in the home of a couple and their two daughters—eighteen and fifteen years old. When the subject of mid-life comes up in the conversation, the wife says, "I've not thought too much about middle age. I guess there isn't too much good to think about after hearing the gripes and groans of those who are a bit older than me." But her husband has a different reaction.

When I ask if they've ever contemplated the possibility that mid-life could bring an easing of the tensions caused by external schedules and obligations, he says, "Oh, yes, I've been thinking about that quite a lot. Frankly, there are some things I'm looking forward to. Our girls have been a delight to us, but they're going to be leaving us soon to develop their own lives. We've already determined that we're not going to hold on to them. We'll send them off when they're ready to go and then [he slyly winks at his wife] we're going to spend a lot of time getting lovey-dovey again."

"Again!" she responds in mock sarcasm. "And when did it stop?" I asked the eighteen-year-old if she ever thought that her parents might enjoy being alone in the same way that she fantasizes being alone some day.

"I never thought about it, but I can see where they'd want more free time" she says. *"They've spent an awful lot of time fitting into our lives."*

The father picks up on his earlier comments again, "We've really enjoyed our family, but many times I've wanted my wife to join me on a business trip or just to go out to eat on the spur of the moment. I guess you could say that, after the girls are gone, we intend to live a lot more spontaneously."

My host has grasped the principle of mid-life release from external pressure. He's careful to make sure that each of us at the table does not think that he feels dissatisfied with his trip to Denver or that he hasn't enjoyed being a parent. But he sees possibilities in a new stage of life that's coming. He obviously doesn't intend to circle anxiously at the wall. He spots something good in the coming new order of things.

His wife acted amused by his comments about being "lovey-dovey again" but my mind holds no doubt that she feels one with him in this expectation of a new and equally enjoyable life-style.

A break in pressure comes from the slowing down of family schedule and the ability to cut down on a heap of obligations one did not previously have the wisdom to exempt from life.

Mother's taxi service finally goes out of business in middle years. Involvements in programs oriented toward children, such as PTA, usually cease. The sheer accumulation of hours spent in the support of child care begins to dissipate.

An emphasis on economy of action may develop in many sectors of life. Decisions should become simpler because of the growing reservoir of past experience. One faces an increasing series of previously experienced challenges that now simply require updating. At mid-life one is familiar with many aspects of life that were previously new or strange and produced much anxiety. After years of trial and error I know now how to do my income tax, how to purchase a new car, what to do when the roof leaks, how to cope with a failure, how to deal with a troubled friendship. Past experience reduces the possibility of such present tensions.

This insight not only reflects common sense; this biblical proverb undergirds it: "The glory of young men is their strength; of old men, their experience" (Proverbs 20:29 TLB). When *old* is equated with *wise* and *experience* and not *has-been,* a new and healthy perspective emerges, and the Bible said it all the time.

Add to these thoughts the possibility of a reduction in the pressure to succeed in the things that one does and to accumulate possessions. For many of us, in the earlier days these formed a key to our sense of selfhood. At mid-life that may no longer be true. Now one can enjoy the pursuit of achievement and the reasonable acquisition of certain things but also be free of *having to have them* in order to experience self-respect. No longer do we determine value by winning or losing. (I remind myself of this every time my son destroys me in a game of Ping-Pong. For him, the game has to be won; for me, the game means a chance for fun and simply being with him.) Freed of the need to win or to own, the mid-lifer may be in an advantageous position to like himself, even—strange as it may seem— enjoy the phenomenon of his emerging self. This point deserves further development. (The converse of this is also sadly true and is reflected in those not happy with self. Thus they must succeed in doing things and acquiring ownership. It's all that's left.)

This possibility of liking oneself leads to a second great opportunity that can follow freely in mid-life. Call it the development of a healthy self-esteem. I'd like to underscore that I'm still talking about *possibility* not *guarantee*.

If I spoke of this possibility to my neighbor, I might mention to her about Saint Peter, who wrote to a lot of young Christians who, through persecution and suffering, slowly lost everything they owned. The apostle had urged them not to panic over things like notoriety or wealth, because he foresaw an ultimate dissolution of material things. His conclusion was, as he looked ahead to an apocalyptic end to all things, "Seeing then that all these things shall be dissolved, what manner of persons ought ye to be. . . ?" (2 Peter 3:11 KJV).

We might modify Peter's principle to fit the situation of mid-life. The question remains basically the same: "Seeing that some of the imagery surrounding youthfulness begins to dissolve, what kind of a person do you discover underneath? What aspects of your personhood now surface? Aspects that were never seen or understood before."

Let me describe a hypothetical couple who purchased land and made plans to build a house. In free time and with available cash, they pour a foundation, frame a structure, and then concentrate upon the roof and siding. They feel concern that the neighbors and those who pass by must find their home acceptable and attractive. A visit to the do-it-yourself home, however, reveals the fact that very little attention has been given to the inside. Once through the front door, nothing but partitions, dangling wires, and insulation meet the eye. Externally, the image appears terrific; internally, there is almost nothing finished.

No doubt many young adults face the same pressure from a spiritual standpoint. Our society looks on the outside images, not the inside. All too often we discover this sad fact only at mid-life. Get busy on the inside *now;* we have wasted too much time.

I'm suggesting that the mid-lifer may stand at the enviable point in life where depth and breadth of being, not the busyness of doing, accumulating, or conforming, can become the major function of living. The emphasis can suddenly rest upon the quality, the wholeness, the maturity of a person, where it should have been in the first place.

The New Testament records the moment when Jesus watched various temple worshipers putting alms in the collection box at the temple entrance. Apparently some loved to make a great carnival out of their giving. The loud jingling of a lot of coins of small denominations gave forth the impression of generosity. But amongst the show-offs came a poor woman whose gift impressed Jesus far more. The dropping of her coin hardly made a sound.

But this woman didn't need sounds, because her strength was measured not in terms of what she had or what image she portrayed to others. She apparently had accepted herself and her limitations. As a whole person, she didn't need any external signs or symbols to complete herself. Upon her Jesus Christ put His stamp of approval.

By principle she says something to the contemporary mid-lifer who looks for possibilities. The confident mid-lifer doesn't have to impress anyone. He or she gains integrity and self-esteem through inner values and pursuits.

No longer needing the symbols and images that once seemed so important, the man or woman at high noon feels free to look inward to discover all that God has placed there. Science bids us look into outer space. I suggest that the mid-lifer can freely embark on a quest for inner space. The God who made the infinitude of outer space may also have made a vast number of potential discoveries within oneself. The writer of the Proverbs wrote: "It is God's privilege to conceal things, and *the king's privilege to discover and invent . . ."* (Proverbs 25:2 TLB, *italics mine*). Seeking concealed treasure in oneself: an opportunity and privilege perhaps best experienced at mid-life.

I take this question of the conquest seriously as I go through the wall of mid-life. I, too, take part in the trip to Denver, and having arrived at the city limits, I remind myself that healthy reactions do not include long looks backward or fearful glances forward. But I don't want anything to do with the campers either. I determine that mid-life will help me discover myself. I want to reveal—as much as possible—the person whom God created when He made me. That unveiling becomes an enhancement as I strip away some of the "stuff" accumulated in younger days, when I had to feel sure that others accepted externals of my life. That "stuff" may consist of some foolish ambitions, debilitating habits, unwholesome attitudes, and a few insipid convictions.

The famous commercial says, "You only go around once in life. . . ." That may be the only truthful thing about that advertising, and it's worth pondering. If I only make the westward trip once, I must make it count. I want to discover the internal self, for there God does his most creative work. The Christian gospel says that God's objective is to make people become progressively more like Jesus Christ. Most of that shaping process occurs internally. Mid-life offers a tremendous opportunity for a lot of that to happen.

My own mid-life quest has begun with a sabbatical leave

from my normal schedule. Convinced that I was like an ocean-going ship whose hull became caked with too many barnacles, I decided to put in for a cleaning.

Such ships go into dry dock, and that's where I went. Asking the board of elders of our congregation for a four-month leave, I broke from normal routines and set out to look inward. I felt convinced that in four month's time I could scrape the hull of my life, overhaul the mental and spiritual engines within, and refocus my navigation instruments on the directions that God had in mind when He made me.

When we first publically announced the sabbatical, my wife, Gail, and I braced ourselves for an avalanche of criticism by people who wouldn't understand what I had in mind. They overwhelmed us, however, with support. Almost every day one or two letters arrived at our home, from members of our beloved Grace Chapel family, encouraging us and applauding my decision. Many affirmed my *courage* in deciding to get away.

Courage? We wondered what kind of courage people thought I exhibited in slipping away from routines. I expected them to think of me as a coward—or at the very least, as quite lazy. Why would they think it courage?

Possibly some sensed my act of stepping back momentarily from my work as an admission that I did not see myself as indispensable in this world? Did they hear me saying the congregation could probably get on without me? Were some people indicating that saying such things takes an element of risk?

How frightening to face one's dispensability. Eda LeShan recalls a day back in the sixties when Mayor John Lindsay tried to solve the great traffic snag back in New York City during a transit strike by going on television and asking all "non-essential workers" to stay home the next day. Nice try, but it didn't work. The next morning a record-setting number of commuters overran the city of New York, all rushing to their jobs in order to indicate that they were essential.

Perhaps some thought me brave to risk proving myself non-essential. This sort of reaction says to me that once again we feel tempted to value what a person *does* rather than what he *is*. What a commentary on the status of our values today!

The number of mid-life men and women who openly admitted envy for my course of action impressed me. "I wish I could do something like that," they'd say. And they really meant it.

Some would have found it impossible, but many others will not try it because new cars, larger homes, higher promotions will always enslave and deny the opportunity to take the time to get in touch with the inner self.

Carl Jung suggests that another opportunity that comes to one in mid-life—high noon—is the chance to discover one's culture. Here we delve into what we might call *avocation,* the pursuit of activities and interests that may not earn money or advance careers but, which lead a person to a whole new level of personal fulfillment.

English psychologist Elliott Jacques studied the lives of several hundred creative people in the history of Western culture. Among the conclusions to which he came was the fact that a significant number of men and women did not produce works of note until after the onset of mid-life. Maybe until these "late bloomers" could establish other more survival-oriented priorities in their lives, their obligations partly restricted them from expressing what they saw in their culture. Perhaps once he completes such priorities, the mid-lifer can begin looking, describing, studying, interpreting, and even remaking what he has discovered.

I see a lovely mother of several children suddenly coming alive to talents for writing poetry and short stories. For many years the drive had been, by necessity, partially shelved because of other selected priorities. Now with some pressures relaxed, her husband encourages her to pursue the expressions of culture. Her poems at first appear in our church paper; then a story runs in her community's newspaper. Now she dares a book-length manuscript that a publisher accepts. Does it really matter if she becomes a famous author? Not as much as it matters that she pursues the opportunities of a new stage of life.

A man I know goes back to college at mid-life to pursue another degree. A new career perhaps? No, he simply wishes to learn some things in an area of knowledge about which he'd always been curious. Someone tackles a Great Books reading program; another relocates in a different country for a year; still another tries a hand at building a house. In each case, a person decides to enjoy the scenery along the road of life, and once having reached Denver, has time to look sideways a bit more frequently.

If I hear Jung correctly, I think he's suggesting that only at mid-life may people stop long enough to discover that life should be lived, not squandered.

I have other reasons for getting excited about mid-life, among them the possibility of a new starting point for those who feel the need to bury crippling failures or consequences resulting from bad choices. In other words, a mid-course maneuver.

I drink coffee with a man who committed himself to the wrong career. Several years of education have put him in a specialized role with which he has grown increasingly resentful.

"What would you have done differently?" I ask. He begins to speak wistfully of teaching as his real love. Having done some of it at a nearby community college, he discovers a joy he'd never known possible. "I'm a natural in the classroom," he says. "Why couldn't I have discovered that before?"

I suggest that change is possible as one enters the mountains of mid-life. His children are finishing college; he doesn't need such a large home or a brand-new car; he and his wife could scale down their standard of living and get by on a teacher's salary.

Now a few years later, after that famous coffee date, my friend teaches in a public-school system. He makes half his former salary, but he feels happy, excited about getting up in the morning.

Elizabeth O'Connor tells the story of Bud Wilkinson, a military officer and later a business executive. He enjoyed all the symbols of success, except fulfillment. One night on a retreat at Dayspring, the church retreat center for Washington's Church of the Savior, Wilkinson seemed to hear a voice speaking within. "Bud, you're a potter, and you always will be."

Taking a cue from the strange message, Bud Wilkinson enrolled in a school of art in downtown Washington, D.C. "The minute my hands touched clay, I knew I was born to shape it," Wilkinson once told me when I had the privilege of briefly meeting him. Soon after, he resigned his position, opened his own studio, and went to work. His wife took a job as a secretary at the National Geographic Society until he could make financial ends meet. A tank commander turned business executive turned potter. A new start! That's possible at mid-life.

People who have failed appreciate the significance of new starts. After I preached a series of sermons on the subject of failure, a man in our congregation invited me to lunch with him. He wanted to share some personal experiences, through which he had traveled, in which the overriding theme had been failure. In a period of thirty minutes, my friend described how he worked his way into a professional cul-de-sac. "I had politicked for certain advancements within my company," he shared with me. "When I knew an interview was coming up, I crammed my mind with every piece of information I thought would impress them. But instead I worked my way into a job situation where sooner or later I would be found out. It becomes immensely difficult to face the fact that you're not equipped to do a job that has turned into the most important thing in your life."

A whole new career opened up for this man. It pays less and draws less attention in terms of social prestige. But he enjoys going to work and doing a job ideally suited to him. The courage for this change and the ensuing jump off the swiftly spinning carousel came in early mid-life. We talk about the job of new starts together, and my lunch companion feels thankful that he leaped at the opportunity to turn a failure into a mid-life success.

A football team plays two quarters of a game and enters the locker room three touchdowns behind. The coach has a big job. In about twenty minutes he needs to convince his team the game is not over, that they may overcome a scoring deficit. How does he do it?

First, he forces the team to acknowledge its mistakes. He puts x's and o's on a blackboard, showing where linebackers were caught out of position and where pass receivers failed to run toward daylight. Then he moves from mistakes to possibilities. New plays, a new game plan. He reminds them that thirty minutes is a long time and that a commitment to excellence can make things work—that the person ready for a new start in the second half can achieve success.

The team cannot always alter the score, but there remains a chance for a try. The God of Jesus Christ has so constructed the scheme of things that great possibilities for new starts appear when one reaches "Denver." I talk with parents who feel they have failed with a child who's grown up to repudiate their God, their value system, their love. They experience a paralyzing sense of defeat. I cannot relieve them of the hurt that they are mother and father to a "prodigal," but I can reaffirm the doctrine of new starts for them both. So we speak of new ways to relate to the rebellious son or daughter, and we move on to new things that could mark the parents' lives and give them a renewed sense of positive contribution in their world.

A man visits with me and shares the resulting grief of a complete misapportionment of his priorities in terms of job, marriage, and relationship to God. The consequences of bad choices now show as the mountains of mid-life loom on the horizon. He feels frightened and desperate enough to talk about it.

Like the football team in the locker room, we analyze where he made the wrong choices. We discuss new game plans, new responses and reactions, new investments of time and energy.

This same mid-life stage that could have been a threat suddenly becomes his opportunity to rearrange things.

Finally, we kneel to pray, and we ask God if He would give this man a chance for a new start. We pray that, as he begins his trek through the mountains, God would reveal the right and proper course. Today, sometime later, I see the score changing in his favor. But that began because he saw opportunities at mid-life as just that—opportunities and not the tragic end to a bad beginning.

In preparation for this chapter I have frequently tried out my parable and its implications to anyone willing to listen. Some candidly suggested that I was rationalizing, trying desperately to find something good to say about mid-life. But follow-up discussions revealed that people began to think more seriously about their victimization by a society that has little to offer the mid-lifer. It was true, they said, that they had been taught to belittle themselves as mentally tired, sexually inept, and physically debilitated. Yes, they received the same message: Avoid the mountains of mid-life at all costs.

Excitingly many of these mid-lifers began to take a whole new look at those mountains. They showed me that it can be done. People can actually stop looking backward, stop circling endlessly at the wall. People can charge into the "mountains" with a sense of anticipation that there exists a God who is a God of dramas—the dramas even of high noon. And when the dramas are over, we will have made greater and more exciting discoveries. The trip to Denver only begins the journey. We must head toward the mountains, where greater dramas await us.

These possibilities are very real to me. I've seen them actualized by people around me, and I'm discovering them for myself. That's what my neighbor has to see also. When I see her again, I'll attempt to tell her about the trip we're all taking to Denver. Perhaps she, too, can begin to affirm the excitement of what may lie in those mountains on the horizon.

Section II

Reflections on Mid-Life Physiology

5

To Catch a Falling
Softball

I faced one of my life's small moments of truth. A swatted softball began its arc, all the time headed toward right field, where I stood, or rather nervously danced, trying to catch it. At stake stood our team's chance to retire the other side in the final inning, my opportunity to gain some admiration from my kids, sitting on the sideline, and the rare possibility of squelching some of those nasty (certainly untrue) rumors that pastors are usually insipid athletes.

It was Sunday-school picnic time. The captains chose teams for the traditional "old men-young men" softball game, and they courteously gave me a harmless assignment to play in the outfield. Someone called the position "roving deep fielder." Since no balls were hit in my direction, I had done minimal damage to our team's scoring interests. But now, at the game's most critical moment, a ball soared my way.

Where was that ball going to come down anyway? I appeared to run sideways, forward, and backward all at once. Now the ball had reached the apex of its climb; it began to descend. In those passing milliseconds my mind began to think simultaneously on two frequencies. One part tried to project a collision course for my glove and the ball, while another part kept asking why this catch seemed so difficult. Why wasn't running, shading my eyes from the blinding sun, judging the ball's trajectory as simple as it once had been. Eyes, feet, arms, and brain seemed to be having a terrible time getting it all together.

I'd once laughed when I heard the tale of a man talking to a friend about his attempts at tennis. "My brain barks out the command to my body: *Run forward rapidly. Start now. Slam the ball over the net. Run quickly back and get ready to do it again!*"

The friend asked, "So what happens then?'

The answer came back, *"Then* my body says, *Who, me?"* Now running frantically toward the ball's landing zone, I couldn't laugh anymore.

In that hair-raising moment I experienced a preview of one of the dramas that awaits the mid-lifer at high noon. *My body's changing on me!* It doesn't quite deliver as it once did. Like a lot of people I may not wish to admit to the changes, but little incidents like that will cause me to face it sooner or later.

Many men and women headed toward the middle years will not want to gracefully give in to the fact of physiological change. I find that I haven't! For men the issue centers generally on strength and agility; for women the issue may be physical appearance. Few of us are well equipped to accept the transitions that will inevitably come. We receive warnings of course, but we can still feel surprised that it's happening to us.

I didn't take my body's first warnings seriously: Are you watching your weight? Enough exercise? Had an EKG lately? Prostate checkups every year after forty (for men)? Pap smear every year (for women)? Hearing and eyes checked regularly? But I realize now that I tended to keep thinking those questions were for other people. Now the plummeting softball rudely confronted me with the fact that the messages had also been addressed all the time in my name.

How do I feel about the abrupt and unavoidable changes I see my body going through? I see a friend from schoolboy days whom I've not seen in fifteen years. Inwardly the shifts in his physical appearance startle me. He looks . . . old, I think. There follows the disquieting realization that my friend is actually fourteen months younger than I am. Does he think the same thoughts about me? Can he see aging in me? Why do I feel concern?

My attitudes about physiological change are being challenged with growing frequency. For example, I have a morning ritual that involves the use of the bathroom scale. Lately, that instrument has presented me with bad news. It won't lie or even exaggerate. It cooperates with my conscience in reminding me of everything I ate the day before—things I should have avoided but didn't. I don't like my scale anymore. It reminds me that the days in which a malt, an extra piece of pie, or a late-night pizza made little difference to my waistline are gone. In other words, I have broadened a bit in the middle now. Middle-aged spread has not remained a fairy tale.

A dour-faced man on television conspires with my bathroom scale and reminds me about another aspect of mid-life change. He keeps advocating some formula that could do wonders, he claims, for my graying hairline. "What gray?" I mutter. "The avalanche of it coating the sides of your head," my wife responds. *So what's wrong with gray?* I wonder. "Battleships and filing cabinets usually get painted gray," I defensively observe. "Not *bright* gray," she responds. The man on the TV thinks I should camouflage the telltale gray; blacken it, he says, so that no one will notice. *Should I be ashamed of gray?* I ask myself.

A magazine that comes to our home each month includes an advertisement designed to appear like a general-interest article. But it's not an article; it's rather a subtle persuasion piece designed to catch my wife's eye and cause her to cover the equivalent of my gray hair: her wrinkles. ("What wrinkles?" she asks.)

It tells you to look youthful. Don't show your age or you're finished! That's the message that filters through. Such an intimidating doctrine can cause young adults to dread mid-life; and it tempts some mid-lifers to look nostalgically backward, mourning what's been irrevocably lost. Somewhere in our Western culture, a lot of people have bought the idea that worthwhile physical beauty belongs only to the young. Believe that, and it will play havoc with your attitude.

The man on TV who wants to cover my gray and the writer in the magazine who wants to erase my wife's wrinkles actually suggest the same thing: They propose a conspiracy against the acts of nature. They suggest that she and I roll back the aging process and pretend to be what we're not. According to them, gray and wrinkles are out. Camouflage is in.

Some of the treatment we give our middle adult bodies reveals our attitudes toward physiological change. If we habitually choose camouflage, we signal our fear and rejection of what's happening to us. If, however, we choose a carefully designed regimen of body care (exercise, rest, diet, and so on) for the purposes of regulating our aging process in accord with good health, we indicate a respect for our aging and self-acceptance. Unfortunately, too many of us choose the former alternative.

Peter Chew, fascinated by mid-life camouflage, quotes John Revson, the cosmetics executive, who explains why male cosmetics are the fastest growing part of his industry:

> Middle-aged men today are buying "male cosmetics" as we're calling them here—or we'll call them "grooming products"—because they're looking for that fountain of youth. Everybody is looking to maintain a youthful image today. Everything in our society is youth oriented.

Eda LeShan would have loved that quote, because it only serves to underscore what she tried to say just a few years ago:

We now live in an age that values only youth. It used to be that to have white hair, a lined face, a bent body was to be respected, even venerated—for a life of hard work. The highest compliment we can be paid today is to be told that we don't look our age. Men and women spend millions of dollars every year on trying to remain youthful and glamorous, untouched by life and aging.

LeShan is quite aware that only in recent times has the pendulum of value swung from the elderly to the youthful. For most of human history the aging man acted as the sage of the village, receiving reverence and admiration. In eras where oral history alone preserved the lessons of the generations, others honored the aged because their accumulation of years meant they possessed maximum wisdom and knowledge.

But in our modern day, all that has apparently changed. Knowledge at least can be taped and heard, filmed and seen, written about and read. Who needs the village elder? Technology has forced the "old man" into obsolescence. The balance of value shifts to the side of the young. But we overlooked that while we may store knowledge, we cannot so contain wisdom. Thus, as the cult of youthfulness steals the edge through technology, it potentially leaves our society virtually bankrupt in terms of wisdom. The aging person not wishing to be identified as old may eschew his or her opportunity to represent wisdom. If no authentic elders remain in the community, we face a famine in terms of wisdom.

Later in her book, LeShan again attacks this tendency within our Western culture:

The American economy, with its dependence on luxury spending, has created a monster in advertising, an environment in which what people look like is far more important than what they really are—where, for example, a Hugh Hefner bunny-type with a full

bosom and a provocative behind, is considered more
sexy than a seasoned woman of forty, who got her
wrinkles and bulges in the course of many years of
sensual appetites being thoroughly explored. The
young boy on horseback or skis who exhales cigarette
smoke in a sexy way is considered the perfect image
of the masculine male, while a man of fifty who has
devoted many years to the careful study of how to
make a woman feel wonderful is judged to be old.

No less disturbed about all of this is Garson Kanin who, although writing of an older period in the aging process (retirement), feels the same discriminatory pressure.

> Youth is big business. Youth is for sale in all de-
> partment stores, in every beauty salon, on far too
> many television commercials. They sell; we buy.
> Why?
> How many men and women have been ripped off
> by the purveyors of anti-wrinkle creams and lotions
> and preparations; or stuff to make eyes brighter, teeth
> whiter, hair thicker, busts bigger, stature taller,
> bodies thinner or fatter? The billions and billions of
> dollars spent on these useless, fruitless products
> might have been spent on something of value.
> When Philippe Halsman came to photograph
> Anna Magnani, he did not want her to be disap-
> pointed by his photographs and so warned, "My lens
> is very sharp, it will show all the lines on your face."
> "Don't hide them," she said. "I suffered too much
> to get them."

The culture-shaped attitudes that rightly disturb LeShan
and Kanin have to be dealt with head-on. If I, as a mid-lifer,
am to overcome negative attitudes about myself and my body,
the kind that engender fear, insecurity, and even inferiority, I
have to know more about myself and these physical changes

going on about me and within me. I must learn what changes I need to *accept* and what processes I can realistically *prevent*. I think of the pursuit of such knowledge as a Christian act.

Saint Paul wrote to the Corinthians "your body is the temple of the Holy Ghost" (KJV). Admittedly, he spoke to a different sort of problem, but the principle he annunciated becomes relevant when we talk of attitude. I think I hear Paul assuming the wonder and beauty of the physical body. In addition, I think his principle implies the need for careful treatment and use of one's body. Obviously Paul feels great respect for God's design of the human body, its capabilities and resilience. He wrote in a nonscientific and nonmedical age, but I'm sure he'd be among the very first to encourage you and me to accept *what* we are, and where we are in each phase of physical growth and development. Given his mind set, I have no doubt that he'd push us to understand all the specifications and performance ratings of the component parts of these "temples" of ours. A review of some of those parts and their potentiality for change at mid-life might prove useful in developing proper attitudes.

Start with certain middle-year *glands,* for an example. No one I can think of knew anything about them in Paul's day, but people nevertheless had to cope with them. Wouldn't the apostle have been fascinated with that collection of tiny hormone-manufacturing centers throughout our bodies that account for many of the changes, urges, appetites, and strengths within us? You and I will never fully understand the dramas of mid-life if we don't master some basic knowledge about our glands.

Most of the glands and their hormonal products that might be particularly germane to the mid-lifer first come in for serious scrutiny when a child reaches the age of puberty. Some glands apparently lie dormant for almost a dozen years after birth. When they finally swing into motion, changes result, for example, in body proportion, sexual interest, food appetites, and appearance. Parents often become confused and frustrated by wide swings in the emotions of their teenagers. Frequent unexplained lows and highs in temperament result. A father wonders how a son or daughter can explode with energy one day and feel listless and apathetic the next. Why? Glands and the novel effect they exert upon the body. The body is not quite used to the impact of some of the powerful products glands inject into the body. To some extent, the initial effect resembles that of a drug.

But in certain conditions and situations the reverse situation may take place at mid-life, playing a new set of tricks upon the body. Now for the first time in twenty-five or thirty years, some of the same glands that originally contributed to the turning of a person from a child to a young adult modify their rates of function; some, in fact, close up shop for good at high noon. The body, now quite used to the functions of these glands, faces a similar challenge to the one it had at adolescence: how to respond to the different realities created by the glands.

If you want some theology behind this kindergarten level endocrinology, let me suggest that the fluctuations of the glands over a life-cycle may be very much a part of God's design in our creation. I think I see God programming our physical bodies in such a way as to drive us into adult actions (away from childhood) at the right time. To get us on the move, he arranged for us to be supercharged with special hormonal fuels. Growth, energy, and even a high level attraction to the opposite sex accelerated just as the Creator designed.

But in another sense God also prefers for us to live on the basis of received knowledge and wisdom. And as we acquire these products of maturity, the once powerful influence of some of the glands may slowly recede. In fact, when Saint Peter writes about people living according to their passions and Saint Paul talks of people "whose God is their belly," they unknowingly describe people, at least in part, overcontrolled by their glands; they've never grown up or matured. An undisciplined person who lives under the persistent dominance of his glands or emotions becomes a danger to himself and society.

Let me note again that if the initial influence of certain glands and hormones marks adolescence, mid-life faces the trauma of some of these same production centers ceasing to function or at least altering their levels of secretion and rates of operation. As there were once adolescent mood fluctuations, there can be some of that again until one's body and mind adjust to the new physiological realities of mid-life. Some reshaping of the body may occur; growing levels of fatigue may result. All sorts of possibilities for change exist, and the more we prepare for them, the less the shock and the greater opportunity for mastering them without undue stress.

I suppose that the glandular changes affecting the human reproductive system get the most attention. Quite possibly the majority of people who considered the topic of this book would have immediately made an association with female menopause and a strange host of modifications tied to sexuality, facing both mid-life men and women. These changes frighten a lot of us. I am obviously not a physician, and cannot speak with medical certitude. But as a pastor I long ago found it necessary to peruse some general knowledge about the dynamics of menopause in order to be sensitive to the pressures and stresses.

The key hormones involved in menopause (and there are several) include estrogen (essentially a female hormone) and testosterone or androgen (essentially a male hormone). Produced by the adrenal gland in small and equal quantities in both male and female, until puberty, these hormones have no significant effect upon us until they begin to flow as a product of the ovaries and the testes, after puberty begins. Other hormones, *gonadotrophins,* secreted by the pituitary gland, trigger the ovaries and testes into action, and result in a whole series of distinct physical changes that define more specifically maleness or femaleness. This combination of hormones will continue to work from puberty until mid-life, when the physiological drama of high noon begins.

When the ovaries and testes begin to function, in early adolescence, they emit significant quantities of their respective hormones and cause characteristics with which we're all familiar; shape of figure, growth of hair on parts of the body, enlargement of genitals and breasts, and because of the female estrogenic secretion, even the tapering off of physical growth, causing women to be smaller in stature than men. The female reproductive cycle of ovulation and menstruation and the male production of sperm and the capacity to discharge it commence.

More important, these same glands that have faithfully produced estrogen and testosterone since puberty may begin to function less consistently, the estrogen secretions becoming increasingly irregular in timing and rate of output, thus affecting a mid-life man or woman in some of the same ways they were affected physically and emotionally at the onset of puberty when all this began. The testosterone production usually remains about the same until a much more advanced age.

We're all aware that menopause appears to be far more a distinct female experience than a male one. The dramatic changes within a woman's body almost all correlate with the cessation of many of the reproductive elements of her system. The "change," as it is more commonly called, includes the conclusion of monthly menstrual cycles and ovulation, and child-bearing days end. But most of us realize it covers more than that.

It takes a certain amount of courage to write about female menopause. Entire books exist on the subject, none of them complete. For who can predict or describe the full combination of possibilities of experience that may come to a woman in mid-life when change of life occurs? It has been reported that 20 percent of all women experience virtually no overt or difficult effects whatsoever during menopause. A much larger percentage report some periodic minor discomfort, while a smaller percentage speak of an incredible mixture of difficulties while their bodies undergo mid-life modification.

Difficulty during menopause usually relates to problems

with estrogen—uneven doses or the absence of the hormone. These may result in sensations such as dizziness, headaches, and even the notorious but not so uncommon hot flashes. Some women also experience secondary effects such as emotional depression, tendencies toward irritability and impatience, and even assorted pains, most real but some psychosomatic.

Women have kidded me about writing on the subject of female menopause. Their comments vary: "What do you know about it?" "You'll have to go through it in order to describe it." "Make sure that you tell people it's a miserable experience!" or, "Tell them that menopause is nothing to worry about; it's a relief!" Who could possibly please all the people who have differing opinions like that?

As a man and as a pastor I have observed some things that I think worth mentioning, however. One of them is that I have no doubt that a lot of women who suffer mid-life discomfort in menopause are suffering real things. Can one find anything more frustrating (and heartbreaking) than to be told that such sensations merely result from an overactive imagination? Many husbands contribute in a destructive way to their wives' sense of well-being by appearing quite unsympathetic to these experiences. A compassionate husband would do well to remain as sensitive as possible to his wife's needs during this period. Again foster open communication in the mid-life marriage.

But an enormous percentage of those women who experience a negative menopause enter mid-life from patterns of spiritual and emotional life that seem to set the stage for these problems. Conversely, those women who have developed strong marriage relationships (if married) possess a high sense of purpose of their lives, enjoy a healthy self-image, and accept circumstances with the determination to draw God's best from them seem to take menopause in their stride. Naturally, we have to allow for some exceptions where physical systems simply go awry, but I think we can make a reasonable case for the fact that a strong, stable life-style creates a context in which a mid-life change will be a trauma of minimal implication.

Dr. Sheldon H. Cherry, who writes at length about the kind of woman who faces menopausal disorder and depression, agrees:

> It is apparent that the degree of the stress in symptomology is directly related to the past emotional and psychiatric situation of the woman. Women who have lived on the borderline of emotional instability for most of their lives seem to have the most difficult times. Those with a history of chronic sexual difficulty usually have menopausal problems. Narcissistic women, women who want to get without giving, women who are immature and childlike, and those who still seek childhood gratification are more likely to have emotional problems. The woman to whom erotic attractiveness was the chief symbol of her personal worth naturally feels a void at this time; the woman with a history of chronic sexual dissatisfaction may suddenly become agitated by the awareness of what she has missed and feel that she can no longer make up for it. The single woman now knows for certain that she can no longer look forward to bearing children; the married woman may feel that her meaningful years are over, that her children and husband are no longer interested in her. Women who lack good friendships, challenging responsibilities, and deep interests in life will naturally suffer more than those women who have made their lives meaningful and whole.

Sheldon's comments startled me because I saw him underscoring some basic Christian truths that the Bible taught twenty centuries before people ever knew about hormones. He's suggesting that there is a basic correlation between the physical functions of our bodies and the spiritual dimensions of our inner spirits. Read Sheldon's words again, and you'll see that he expects more than average mid-life adjustment problems for women whose life-styles have been marked with self-centeredness, poor-quality relationships, less than godly goals and purposes in life, and who exploited their own sexuality to achieve personal worth.

His insight illustrates why, as a pastor, I even dare to write a chapter in which I attempt some general physiological descriptions. Because I see a Christian implication in almost every physical change. Assuming physical normality, mid-life physiological changes can be experienced with minimal stress *if* the person who possesses them has spent earlier adult years learning respect for the body God gave, discipline in response to drives and appetites, and the development of an inner spiritual nature, so that by mid-life convictions and values draw and control him or her.

When I preach on Sunday or lead a Bible study that expresses the need for spiritual cultivation and discipline, I do not simply aim at getting people to become "good Christians." The implication of my thrust usually extends to every part of our beings—even to the way we will respond at mid-life to the machinations of our endocrinal system and its necessary fluctuations.

Back to menopause. Debate continues as to the role of estrogen within the female body. Loss of estrogen can have sexual implications, for example. The tissues and walls of female genitals can grow somewhat thin and atrophied. Obviously that could have an effect upon sexual desire at mid-life. The possibility of genital discomfort always exists, and that could lead a wife to possess diminishing interest in sexual relationship. One thing leads to another, and the conclusion is frustration, possible growing distance between husband and wife. Finally, silence! If a man seems unable to invite responses from his wife, he may feel tempted to generalize in his mind that menopause has cost his marriage its sexual dimension. He may begin to doubt his own attractiveness as a man, and this lays the groundwork for serious sexual temptation through alternative relationships.

A wife who, not fully prepared or informed, does not understand the changes within her may feel no less frustration. If she puts off consulting a physician (and many do), if she keeps thinking that things will improve within a day or so (and many think that), if she begins to resent her husband because she feels that he is insensitive to her problem, the marriage will quickly begin to hurt from her perspective also. Counsel and prescription from a competent physician can often bring a high percentage of these problems to a satisfactory resolution. That many women fail to consult their doctors on these matters probably results from their ignorance of potential solutions or a subconscious desire not to solve the problem, thus using it as an excuse to avoid sexual intimacy in a lukewarm marriage.

The preliminary answer for both a troubled husband and wife facing such trauma would have included preparation and communication. Preparation in that they both understand long ahead of time what might happen as the result of menopausal functions and communication that overcomes suspicion and neglect.

I have visited with too many men and women about the tragic consequences of ignorance not to know that we're thinking through a very serious problem here. As I see it we can solve this problem in the adult years *before* the drama unfolds. In short, the marriage that thrives at mid-life probably thrived in the prenoon hours.

Is there a male menopause? If so, most people agree that it affects one more psychologically than physiologically. Certain hormonal fluctuations can cause hair loss, especially on arms and legs. More than a few of us have found hair in the drain of the bathtub that we'd thought was safely attached to the top of our heads. I once wondered if the Lord keeps an accurate tabulation of hairs of our head and updates the count after every shower.

Mid-life may result in a slight decrease in the male sperm rate, but certainly not to an extent that would prevent the normal male from fathering children. Deuteronomy 34:7 indicates that even at the age of 120 Moses was capable of fathering a child. Researchers usually discover a modest decline in the frequency of mid-life male sexual activity, but find it hard to pin this down to any one reason. At any rate it usually proves insignificant if one's marriage and sense of personal well-being remain healthy.

The male counterpart to the fear that some women have of a bad menopause might focus on the problem of mid-life impotence. Physicians agree that the root of most cases of impotence tend to center more in the mind than in the physiology of the male. Some of the more common origins include increasing stress because of accumulating personal problems, preoccupation with vocational challenges, increasing fatigue, or a strange self-feeding fear of loss of masculinity. Sexual difficulties existing within the marriage and enhanced through the effects of a wife's menopausal experience might tie in with the last fear. Again, as in the case of a woman's attitude, the body functions best when the mind and heart remain submissive to God's order of things.

I suspect that any doctor would tell a mid-life man to expect a few times when his body would not respond to sexual opportunity. The doctor would doubtless counsel treating such experiences as insignificant. To become possessed with fear and create a mental and emotional crisis out of one or two cases of periodic failure might escalate impotence through preoccupation with the wrong matter.

Some men remain unaware that certain medications for high blood pressure, for example, can cause a decrease in male sexual ability. It also might be worth adding that excessive drinking of alcoholic beverages (not an uncommon matter for a troubled mid-lifer) can contribute to impotence. But beyond this, there seems to be no reason why a man approaching his middle years cannot expect an uninterrupted experience of sexual activity.

Students of adult development have found that the sexual

dimensions of marriage can in fact provide increasing satisfaction for both husband and wife. With the absence of fear over an unwanted pregnancy and the growing opportunity for privacy, healthy marriage partners can look forward to an acceleration of satisfaction and delight in their middle years.

Let me confess once again how hard I find it to write about these things. I suspect I fear that the reader will lose interest and dismiss these paragraphs as a juvenile hygiene lesson. But I remember so many husbands and wives who have ignorantly faced these matters and, misunderstanding events within themselves, have slipped into bitterness and resentment against each other and doubt about themselves. Since their pride causes them to resist taking their questions and frustrations to a trusted pastor or a capable Christian counselor, they suffer in stony silence, unwilling to seek out the origins of the matter. The consequence is a sexless marriage, with dwindling affection. Slow and painful destruction of relationship and personhood occurs. And all too often the inception of it all rests with a few glands which, in the natural course of life, made some changes.

I discover that apart from "attitude" physicians have very few helpful answers for suffering mid-life women. Great question marks about the unwise use of estrogen artificially introduced into the system remain. There is greater attention being given to the incredible increase in premature female hysterectomies implemented to solve many problems of immediate discomfort.

Not enough is said about the great shock a hysterectomy is to the female system. I doubt many men appreciate how strongly most women feel when they have to face the fact that their bodies can no longer produce children. Perhaps a woman does not want more, but most feel authentic knowing that at least the possibility of childbearing remains.

The one biblical illustration that approximates what I'm saying is the story of Hannah and Elkanah. Elkanah's love for Hannah is indisputable, but at first he seems to have been less than understanding about Hannah's struggle. "Isn't my love good enough?" he asks. You want to grab Elkanah by the arm and tell him a few things that many men have a difficult time understanding. Today some men seem liable to view hysterectomies or even premature menopause as an advantageous thing for their wives. Their pragmatic perspective centers on the preclusion of pregnancy. They need to see, however, a much more broad and basic issue: how a woman might see herself. A needless hysterectomy or an early menopause is not a matter to be treated lightly or flippantly.

The physicians with whom I visit agree that in those cases where menopause becomes a difficult experience because of uncooperative glands, the only answer lies in a sensitive and communicative husband-and-wife team fighting out the period of stress together. No doubt a tender and caring love can minimize much of the problem and its symptomology. If the question of the glands is medical, the question of attitude in facing what the glands do can be certainly pastoral. That's where I got into all of this.

That Sunday-school-picnic softball nears the ground now. If the crowd, which includes my wife and kids, screams for me to catch it, I don't hear it. I strain with every ounce of consciousness to compute the point of impact. The pastor–author–mid-life husband and father is, at least for this moment, nothing but a ball player. He admittedly takes the role far too seriously, but right now I must catch the ball.

One of the reasons I am struggling to catch up to the ball has to do with the mid-life effect upon my nervous system. It may not normally receive the attention the endocrinal system gets, but it is nevertheless there, and it also is undergoing transition. My nervous system has slowed down in terms of reaction time. That's one reason why I was late in responding to the crack of the bat.

For example, my eyes probably focus on distant and peripheral objects just a bit more slowly than they used to. It's not noticeable (until you try to catch a softball after ten years of athletic retirement) except for, perhaps, a bit of eye strain, since the eyes now work just a bit harder in the course of a day.

My hearing will probably lose a few percentage points of former efficiency also. Again, for most of us, the slight loss seems barely perceptible. Unconsciously we will begin to strain just a bit more to pick up sounds we once took for granted. We'll not know we're doing it usually. The evidence will be a greater fatigue at the end of a day. I may find myself even a bit more irritable than in younger years, because I must concentrate more on things that I once used to pick up with greater ease.

I may discover myself—and I do—becoming oversensitive to the noise my children generate in the backseat of a car on a trip. Even my wife is surprised at my attitude and says so. "They're only having fun," she says. She's right; why am I wrong?

Perhaps the answer lies in the fact that this nervous system of mine now has to work harder gathering its visual and auditory data as I drive. Deep in my mind where I process all this "input," every second, I experience a rejection of extraneous noises and movements. My irritability is part of my unconscious need to concentrate more. I need to understand that; so must my kids. If I do not understand it, I may then realize that all irritability isn't simply a spiritual problem. While attitude and temperament affect my reaction, it is also part of the aging process.

Let me hasten to underscore that these changes for most people are usually minimal. Normally we will only see evidence of them in terms of fatigue or irritability. But as we grow older, we grow wiser. We may not need all the hearing and seeing ability we once did when we were less experienced—unless of course we are in a Sunday-school-picnic softball game. Then we need everything we can get.

Mid-life will probably see some change in my dermatological system—specifically my skin. Skin, my friend, the doctor, tells me, is one of my body's most incredible substances. It has life, elasticity, amazing endurance. Skin is not replaced at the parts counter at Sears. It actually replaces itself. And every square inch of our skin does indeed wear out, usually over a period of seven years. All of us have seen the minor miracle of healing when we've cut a finger. Within days the skin replaces itself and most likely erases the wound without so much as a scar.

But a mid-lifer will probably see the first signs of his dependable skin losing some of its resilience and elasticity. The fabric of flesh that for so many years remained tightly wrapped about his skeletal structure will begin to loosen just a bit, like the overused elastic in the band around my bathing suit. The consequence is seen in wrinkles, sags, and even bulges.

That's partly why my youthful figure slowly abandons me. The skin about my waist simply won't cooperate in holding my eating excesses in. I will have to begin in mid-life to cooperate with my skin rather than asking too much from it.

Skin that stretches just a bit causes facial lines, sagging flesh along the chin or throat. The breasts of a mid-life woman may lose some firmness; unwatched thighs can become like saddlebags. Most of this doesn't have to happen to the mid-life person who watches both diet and exercise.

If you feel edgy about all of this skin business, then let me admit that I do, too. Some people go to extremes, however. Today increasing numbers of women *and* men pay out enormous sums of money to have breasts surgically treated, skin pulled tightly back to cheeks and chins. Lost hair is sometimes replaced through expensive transplants. Today some men even pay for artificial chest hair. Perhaps one advertising slogan I recently saw sums it up: "Let your skin do the lying for you."

I don't feel right in condemning these things, but I do want to ask what one is thinking about if he or she feels it necessary. Is it done out of fear, insecurity, reluctance to admit to the aging process? Is it in some cases an admission of inadequacy in the inner person? Does it betray worry over a marginal marriage or the loss of what some call sexual appeal?

I mean this list of transitions in the mid-lifer's physical world to be illustrative and not exhaustive. Many things could have been spotlighted. We should probably know something, for example, about the effect of calcium loss, which might invite backaches or forms of arthritis. An overtaxed respiratory system will retaliate with extended huffing and puffing and accelerate the problems of heart stress. We should think a bit about the aging heart and the fact that in our culture it receives less and less exercise in most mid-life bodies. Thus it begins to lose some of its earlier capacity to perform under great pressure. There are so many things worth mentioning, but the even larger question is how are we going to live with these realities in mind?

Dr. Kenneth Pelletier in a recent *Psychology Today* article made the following observation:

> During recent years, four disorders—heart disease, cancer, arthritis, and respiratory diseases such as bronchitis—have become so prominent in the clinics of the USA, Western Europe and Japan, that they are known as "the afflictions of civilization." Their prevalence stems from poor diet, pollution, and, most important, the increased stress of modern society.
>
> No one can avoid stress; the wear and tear of stress is part of the cost of living. But for many of us, that cost has become too high. Modern man faces more daily pressures, such as the unrelenting demands of the clock, than have people at any other time in history, and the effect is often devastating. *Our bodies start in late adolescence to accumulate the effects of stress that will surface as disorders when we are in our 40's and 50's.*

Dr. Pelletier's comments justify for me the fact that a Christian pastor needs to talk to people about things such as their endocrinal, nervous, and dermatological systems, because Dr. Pelletier says that the man or woman who has allowed his or her life to come under undue stress in earlier years pays heavily for it in middle years. Such stress often results from failure by a person to order his life according to God's design for human existence.

No evidence exists that Jesus ever faced a crisis for which He was unprepared. When the potential of stress stood in the offing—decisions to be made, people faced, hard words said, even the crucifixion—Jesus was always ready. He'd rested, He'd prayed, He'd positioned Himself in each situation so as to master the crisis, gaining whatever His Heavenly Father intended to be the outcome. You never see our Lord rattled, and, if He had lived on earth through mid-life, we might reasonably assume that the physical changes would have had minimal effects upon him. The lesson of Jesus' life-style is worth pondering. Live according to such dimensions, and the body will not be foolishly taxed to the point where it begins to betray us at mid-life.

How can the mid-lifer face the basic physiological drama at high noon? I perceive three possible alternatives. The mid-lifer can attempt to *fight* the changes (we've already talked a bit about that: camouflage). Second, the mid-lifer could in despair *surrender* to the changes. Or, finally, he or she could *cooperate* with changes which God apparently intended to naturally happen to us.

We've talked enough about the first two alternatives. They're unfortunate. But the third is distinctly Christian. Let me develop this idea by suggesting that our ability to cooperate with change seems to hang on two major matters of conviction: our view of physiological change (physiological transition) and our view of death (physiological termination).

Saint Paul says nothing specific that I know of on the subject of mid-life. But he does say something about transition and termination in, what I think, are definite physiological terms. Let me give you two Pauline quotes:

So we do not lose heart. Though our outer nature [our bodies] is wasting away, our inner nature [our spirits] is being renewed every day.

2 Corinthians 4:16 RSV

[Speaking about the possibility of his own execution at the hand of Nero in Rome] I am hard pressed between the two [living or dying]. My desire is to depart and be with Christ [termination], for that is far better. But to remain in the flesh [in other words, keep on living] is more necessary on your account [the people to whom he was apostle-pastor].

Philippians 1:23, 24 RSV

The first quote illustrates Paul's view of his own physiological transition. He has obviously accepted the fact that his body is not eternal, that it will not always retain a high level of energy or attractiveness that it had in more youthful days. He accepts this; he does not resent it. Why?

Let me answer my own question by first observing that when he wrote those words, Paul wrestled with what motivated him as an apostle. He was in his later middle years and quickly realized that the center of gravity in his life had shifted in preoccupation with things physical to things spiritual. For Paul, the integrity of the inner spirit had become the important thing. In other words, he was inwardly directed. Reality for Paul radiated from *in* to *out,* not *out* to *in.*

Paul indicates *change* in his life on two levels: the *physiological level* of change, which we've already discussed, and the *spiritual level,* which he would call maturing in his personal knowledge and awareness of Jesus Christ. I can't imagine Paul being upset if you commented on the fact that his hair was graying or even disappearing. Wrinkle lines or a modest spread at the waist would not disturb him. But he would have been deeply impressed if you had seen no change in his development of personhood according to the character of Christ. That was where he learned to put his priority.

The aging apostle would have found it easy to relate to theologian William Newton Clarke's poem:

> Gone, they tell me is youth,
> Gone the strength of my life,
> Nothing remains but decline,
> Nothing but age and decay.
>
> Not so! I am God's little child,
> Only beginning to live.
> Coming the days of my prime,
> Coming the strength of my life,
> Coming the vision of God,
> *Coming my bloom and my power.*

Some people do not see transition the way Paul saw it. What have they done that makes things different, that causes them to fear and fight change? The answer, I think, lies in their attempt to dislodge God from His rightful position in the center of their world. The theologian notes that God is immutable, that is to say unchanging. As such He is the only permanent, unchanging being. "Jesus Christ," the writer to the Hebrews said, "is the same yesterday, today, and forever."

In practical implication of this theology, the unchanging God can reach out to control my personal and physiological changes and their effects when permitted by me. The God of heaven designs change, and I need not live in paranoiac fear if I believe that. A famous dancer insures her legs for a million dollars. They are the center of her well-being. No legs, no income, no reason for being. Change frightens her. That's not how God meant us to live!

If I deny the existence of an immutable God at the center of my universe, then I can only afford changes that work to my benefit. I must avoid, camouflage, or lie about changes that threaten my position, my strength, my security. And if I find that impossible, despair lurks just around the corner.

Again, Paul did not feel intimidated by physiological change because it reminded him that he was drawing closer and closer to a point within eternity in which there would "be no crying, no pain, no mourning anymore."

When we accept change and shift our spiritual center of gravity in life from the "outer nature" (the physiological) to the "inner nature" (the spiritual), both dimensions (the inner and the outer) of ourselves benefit. We come back to Dr. Pelletier's comments about the effects of stress upon the mid-life body, and we're back to what a host of physicians such as Sheldon Cherry have said about menopause: Young-adult life lived according to Christian dimensions gives an enormously increased chance of a healthy mid-life.

One of the most enthusiastic Christians of the twentieth century, Methodist evangelist and missionary E. Stanley Jones fully believed in this "whole man" principle: Our bodies respond to our Christian faith through and through.

> Every mental and moral and spiritual attitude that upsets the health and rhythm of the body is unChristian. Not one single authentic Christian attitude interferes with or upsets the body. Call the roll of the emotions, the thinking, the attitudes, the actions that produce personality upset and disrupted living, and what is the list? Fear, resentment, guilt, self-preoccupation, a sense of inferiority, refusal to accept responsibility, dishonesty, quarrelsomeness, negativism, pessimism, hopelessness, retreat from life, refusal to cooperate, sexual impurity, anger, jealousy, envy, pride, mammon, criticism, backbiting, hate, and a lack of love. And every single one of them is unChristian, with no exception.
>
> Now call the roll of the emotions, the thinking, the attitudes that produce harmonious, adjusted, created

personality, and what do you have? Love, apprecia-
tion of others, service, acceptance of responsibility,
willingness to cooperate, sex purity, forgiveness from
God and forgiveness to man, goodwill to all classes
and races, outgoingness, honesty, the absence of inferiority and superiority, optimism, hope, faith. Every
single one Christian! Some Christian principles and
attitudes may be twisted and made into something
other than Christian, but if it is truly Christian, it is
constructive and health-giving and healing.

I hear Stanley Jones telling us that our bodies have been
built to last a lifetime when exposed to a Christian life-style. If
our inner nature grows, then our outer nature will most likely
respond with maximum health at all ages. But if the preoccupation of a person centers on the outer nature, the inner nature
will shrivel and the outer nature ironically will ultimately suffer severe consequences.

Stanley Jones made this same point another way when he
quipped, "You are responsible for your own face after the age
of forty." The point? Our faces tend to mirror what we are
within ourselves—the inner nature.

The inner nature, when tuned to the unchanging center of
all creation—the God of Jesus Christ—will make possible a
personal life experience that minimizes stress and its destructive effects, a mental outlook that does not fear or reject
change, and a physiological state of health that is not abruptly
modified at mid-life. *That's healthy transition.*

The second quote from Saint Paul refers to physiological termination: the fact that each of us is going to die. The middle
years bring most people face-to-face with death, usually for the
first time. Older loved ones are dying; some friends may die
prematurely; we sense that our bodies are beginning to die.
From somewhere within us, the very first death-oriented
thoughts begin to percolate up to our consciousness: "I'm
going to die someday. I don't know how, where, or when. But

sometime from this very second on, I am going to face death."
That irresistible fact has driven many mid-life men and women
through brief periods of depression.

We might object to mid-life physiological transition because
it affirms our future termination. In rejecting transition, we attempt to deny or roll back that inexorable forward progress.
When outside circumstances and physiological change reminded Paul of the coming termination of his earthly life, he
was forced to come to grips with how he felt about it. The conclusion he came up with was that death didn't bother him at
all.

Do you suppose that dying bothered him a bit? There are
very few pleasant ways to die. Fearing dying is one thing, however; fearing the reality of death is another. Paul definitely did
not fear death.

If we fear death, the effects of that phobia will first appear at
mid-life. It is possible that we will actually accentuate some of
the physiological struggles of transition because our fear of termination will fixate sharply upon every sign that death is coming. I don't think therefore that I stretch the point when I
suggest that the struggles and fears of many mid-lifers may
directly relate to how they feel about death.

A physician with much experience with terminal patients,
Dr. James A. K. Boyd has some helpful things to say on this
subject. Speaking on the high percentage of people who fear
their own terminations, Boyd says:

> We fear death in direct proportion to what we feel
> we will lose by it. The person who lives to amass
> things and dominate people has a great deal to lose
> by dying. His control of all of this will end abruptly.

"Loss of control." I read that and say, "Where have I heard
that before?" I heard it, or a version of it, from many people
musing on the symptoms of life at middle years. "Things seem
to be getting out of control," they say. Is that the first premoni-
tion of what death is like?

I think Dr. Boyd tries to make the point that those of us who frantically hold on to our outer natures and things about us fear death. And those of us who fear death are going to resent the transitions of mid-life. This violent and ugly circle spins faster as the years advance.

But listen again to Boyd as he points out why Christianity makes such good sense:

> ... the Christian who surrenders control and gives away his life daily, knows at death that he has nothing to lose and everything to gain. His experience will have taught him that it is in losing his life that he ultimately finds it.

That's exactly the point Jesus Christ tried to make a hundred times with His disciples. It's the point Paul is making when he writes to the Philippians the words we recorded before. "If I continue to live," he says, "I'll give my life to you. If I die, my life goes to be with Christ." Paul can't lose!

Having established this point that death means the surrender of control and that people who fear death fear losing control, Boyd goes on to an astonishing conclusion:

> Christians are called upon to undergo a control-surrendering, death-like process. The more a Christian learns to trust God in this kind of dying—relying on God as an active, dependable force in his life—the more he will be willing to accept his physical dying, the ultimate surrender, entrusting his soul back to the faithful Creator.

That's hard enough to grasp, but the implication is even more mindboggling. Boyd, one more time:

> For the Christian, then, death ought to be an integral part of living—not just its terminal event. Far from being morbid, the perspective of being a living

sacrifice provides genuine purpose and fulfillment in
this life while giving the believer a hope for the next.

And that is the point of this chapter. That transition (mid-
life change) is a reminder of termination (death). But we actually die a little bit each day. And in the face of approaching
termination, we do as Paul did: We give ourselves to Christ,
and we therefore give ourselves to others. The result? Termination holds no fear; transition loses its sting. Each change simply reminds us that the presence of Christ comes closer, that
eternity is one rung more approximate. Hitting the bottom line,
the Christian knows no such thing as termination. Death itself
is actually the point of transition, a change, from the limits of
earthly life to the maximums of eternal life.

The softball at the Sunday-school picnic now falls inches
away from my outstretched glove. Through sheer determination, I am almost there. Roving deep fielders do not have time
to theologize when the final out of the game rests in their
hands. But if I have thought through the issues of transition
and termination in earlier, quieter moments and made commitments to the Lord of the universe that proliferate through
my inner and outer life, then perhaps I will not be unduly hu-
miliated if I cannot catch the ball; nor will I be overinflated
with youthful pride if I catch it. Set in the perspective of life's
realities, it is, in fact, *just* a ball game. And if my mid-life limitations cause our team to lose, what does it matter? There is always another Sunday-school picnic next year.

The ball has come a long way from home plate. And I have
traveled a long distance to the place where it will land. I feel
tired, out of breath, and unfamiliar with the borrowed glove on
my left hand. But amidst such limitations, I've apparently done
something right. Because I suddenly feel the ball smack the
webbing of the glove, and when I look over my shoulder, a second later, to see if I've dropped it, I cannot find it on the grass.
Only then do I dare to believe that I am the Sunday-school
picnic hero. When I look in the pocket of the glove, there it is:

that dumb, inanimate softball for which I have risked my mid-life bones, my out-of-condition muscles, and my athletic reputation.

As my team leaves the field, I run toward the bench, with the ball in hand. I try to act as if it were an effortless catch. But inside I still reflect on how close I came to disaster. Then I hear my kids yell, "Great going, Dad!" and the team captain say, "Will you be back again next year?" and my friend, the physician, snort, "You're out of shape, pastor; come in to my office Monday; I want to put you on an exercise program."

Section III

Reflections on Mid-Life Vocation

6
It's a Lot More
Than a Job!

Among the topics that titillate my curiosity is that of anyone's vocation. Sooner or later I usually ask a new acquaint-
ance, "What do you *do* that's important to your life?" I get a
surprising array of answers. But I'm really pursuing insight
into a person's vocation.

As a category of life, vocation points up what men and
women *do* as the central activity of their adult lives for the
purposes of maintaining a standard of living or giving vent to
creative or constructive instincts or—in some cases—gaining
the satisfaction of having made some contribution to society.
That latter purpose probably ranks among the very highest
motivations that our individual vocational choices can reach.

I don't get uniform answers to my questions about vocations.
One man, perhaps misunderstanding me, even told me that *his*
vocation was none of my business. Perhaps he worked for the
Mafia or the CIA? The responses of most people usually fall
into one of three levels when they talk about what they do.
Some view their work in terms of what they get out of it: a
salary, a position, some sort of long-term security. Another

level of answer comes from those who are content simply to describe the activities that comprise their job such as building homes, selling insurance, driving a bus, or running a medical laboratory.

A third level of response to vocational questions emphasizes what people think they give to their world. Sometimes it adds something of how they envision their growth as human beings and increasing awareness of people and realities about them. They might even see their vocations in terms of achieving a particular purpose that God seems concerned about. This third level is the deepest or the highest of the three because it begins to explore one's spiritual evaluation of doing. Dealing on that level often indicates satisfaction of achievement or contribution as a reward, instead of financial gain. Admittedly, some vocations lend themselves quite readily to this third-level description. But I hope I am not supremely idealistic when I confide my conviction that all vocations ought to be describable and definable in these higher terms.

In and around the high noon of life, most of us begin to enter a period of concentrated self-examination on the matter of the vocational questions. And this quest for certain answers almost never parallels the type of questions we've asked of others and ourselves in earlier years. The vocational answers one seeks at mid-life tend to be found not on the first two levels I previously mentioned—that of *getting* and *doing*—but rather at the third level, the one I suggested to be the most noble. Call that the level of *meaning* or *significance.*

I suspect that this new mid-life quest results from a spiritual force resident within every one of us, which exerts stronger and stronger authority in our thought processes, unless, of course, we've deliberately chosen to suppress it. God set it in motion when he created us. This divinely designed curiosity shows itself if we choose a spiritual or inner orientation in our lives. And if we've not selected such an orientation, this spiritual force will often leap to the surface on its own in a time of crisis, at a moment when we sense our own weakness or vulnerability or at an uneasy interval when we begin to sense that the process of life has a point of terminus. On such occasions we are more apt to ask if what we have done in our lives counts for anything. Have we really made a mark of any kind that will survive us? That a person has any desire to make and leave a mark in this world is a testimony to his or her higher level of existence, created in God's image. For the large majority of us, this profound issue reaches prominence at mid-life.

That released force pushes us to pose questions such as, "What am I doing with my life?" or, "Who in this world is better because of me?" or, "What's going to be left behind when I die?" or, "Could I have done more ... or better?" or, "Is it too late to change?"

The handling of those questions or variations of their themes constitutes the essential vocational drama of mid-life.

I believe that there is a theological base to this vocational drama. The Bible indicates that deep in the spiritual "genes" of our lives, the creating God has placed a thirst for both significance and approval to go along with the natural and spiritual gifts (or abilities) that he has given to every person. Ultimately, an estimate of our significance as persons and a statement of approval for what we've done is supposed to come from God Himself, when we each appear before His judgment seat to account for what we've done with what we've got. Saint Paul repeatedly taught this to young Christians.

Typically many of us substitute the approval of our peers or our systems (political, corporate, and so on) for that which we were designed to seek from God. And in doing so we drift further and further away from calibrating the choice and conduct of our vocations according to criteria laid down by our Creator. By way of illustration, I think I hear Nixon aide, Jeb Stuart Magruder acknowledging such a substitution when he said to Judge John Sirica on the day of his sentencing for Watergate illegalities, "Somewhere between my ambition and my ideals, I lost my ethical compass. I found myself on a path that had not been intended for me by my parents or my principles—or by my own ethical instincts. It has led me to this courtroom."

But what frequently triggers a return to the issues of significance and approval is a growing awareness of an eternal dimension to our lives and a parallel awareness of the ending of this temporal one. And such a context of thinking slowly emerges at mid-life. We should never feel surprised when it appears before us as if staring us right in the face.

This emergent quest for quality in vocation or for significance and meaning in life relates strongly to the fact of accountability to God. Jesus alluded to it when he told the story of a wealthy landowner who left three of his top managers with large sums of money when he left on a long trip, telling them simply, "Use this wisely until I return." Two of the three did; the third simply buried his cache of cash in order to return it intact to the boss upon his homecoming. The other two took some risks, multiplied their assets, and amassed a lot to show for their activities when their master opened the books. Our Lord indicates that the nobleman became outraged over the act of burying the money by the third man. Conversely, the other two were handsomely rewarded. One gets the feeling that the nobleman might have felt more pleased if the third man had lost the money in honest investment risks, rather than burying it.

In a culture where the emphasis can easily provoke us to ask vocational questions on the level of getting rather than giving, we easily tune out the issue of significance and approval and replace it with the questions "What's in it for me and how far can I go to get society's approval [rather than God's]?" But if the spiritual questions ever arise, they'll probably do so at mid-life, and as I said, the drama centers on how those questions will be asked and what we'll do with the answers.

I have frequently pondered the old fable in which a sidewalk superintendent asked three workmen what they were doing. The first responded, "I am laying stone," a second, "I am erecting a wall," but the third said, "I am building a great cathedral." All three were doing the same thing, but they had surprisingly different perspectives.

The summer our New Hampshire saltbox get-away home was constructed, my wife and I watched an old bricklayer build a fireplace chimney right up through the cathedral ceiling of our living room. The man we employed seemed a master at his craft, and I tried to tell him so one day. Admiring his finish work I said, "This chimney is the product of a man who really knows what he's doing. It's a work of art. We'll enjoy it for a lifetime and think good thoughts about you. I hope you get satisfaction out of a project well done."

I felt disappointment at his response to my affirmation. "It's only a job," he commented. He wasn't trying to be modest; he meant what he said. I had hoped to find a positive kind of pride in his attitude about his work, a sign that he, too, felt good about completing something of professional excellence. I suppose I looked for some sort of romantic dimension to his work, some expression of his personhood that he might have incarnated into the chimney. But it wasn't there! He felt no transference between him and what he'd done. He left behind no deliberate statement of his existence. He'd simply done a job.

When I speak of romance, I expect that one might want to leave his or her initials in an obscure corner of the hearth, so as to leave behind a statement of identity, much like an artist who affixes a name to the bottom of a canvas. But the only place my bricklayer friend cared to see his name was on the check we'd given him for getting the chimney up through the roof.

I left that conversation feeling sorry for the man and wondering how many other millions of people (honest and hardworking to be sure) feel that their vocations are "just a job." Surely, this man must have begun his vocation with some sort of enthusiasm and expectation. What was on his mind the first day he reported as an apprentice, with a new trowel in hand? When did the challenge of laying brick and creating something beautiful become routine and mechanical? Did he ever wrestle with the purpose of his work, its significance within the community of human beings and what it might mean to God? If he ever seriously came to grips with these matters, I suspect it might have occurred during the middle years of his life. Apparently, he didn't emerge at the other end of mid-life with a solid answer. So our chimney became just another job.

Yale professor Daniel Levinson has spent many years studying the changing attitudes of men about themselves and the world in which they live as they age. He has made some profound discoveries about the almost uniform reactions of mid-life men as they take hard looks at their vocational settings. He notes Carl Jung's original insight that only in the earliest adult years (what Levinson calls "the novice years") and then again in the mid-life years can most people have either the time or the inclination to evaluate their vocations in terms of choices made, quality achieved, or satisfaction received. I'm not sure I completely agree with Jung about the earliest adult years. The modern emphasis upon "career" may have replaced the idealism to make a mark that Jung saw in his generation. But I willingly stand by the conviction that the real spiritual issues of vocation rarely reach the surface until high noon, as Jung has said. If earlier than that, almost certainly commitment to Christ has caused us to move in that direction.

Can I suggest that we call this third-level vocational quest "an affair of the spirit" (my own term)? As I've already observed, their origin is in the spiritual "genes." These questions cannot come from a calculating mind bent upon materialistic acquisition. Jung and Levinson found that at certain times of life we see our vocation as an affair of the spirit. The first time may occur when we begin to brood on what we might become. The second time takes place when we reach a point where we determine if the original intentions had any validity.

When Levinson speaks of the affair of the spirit, he employs the concept of *the Dream* (a word which he purposely capitalizes). He sees much of one's vocational life as revolving around that Dream. The Dream usually formulated in early adulthood is tested at mid-life, and therein lies Levinson's concept of what I call the vocational drama: the testing of the Dream.

When he talks of the Dream, Levinson makes several interesting observations. He says, for example, that the earliest Dreams of young men (he did not research this in women) are usually ill-defined, outlandishly inflated, and usually too broad or sizable to reach. The later in adult life they formulated this Dream, the more practical the Dream seemed.

Levinson also discovered that men who for various reasons never really formulated a Dream tended to live lives of general disorder and inconsistent behavior, drifting from job to job and dealing relatively superficially with their own senses of self-worth.

Then again, the fact that the Dream tends to "tyrannize" most men, especially in the early years of adulthood, impressed Levinson. The Dream can push and prod a person to extraordinary levels of achievement. It can—and often does—crowd out other priorities such as family, physical health, and even one's spiritual life. An extreme example of this, I suppose, sprung out of a conversation I had one day with an auto-parts dealer who had just cheated a customer by selling him a used part for his car, while representing it as a new one. When I asked him how he justified it, he said, "I would do anything for a buck." It speaks to the focal point of *his* Dream.

As I said, Levinson didn't study women, but if he had, I'm sure he would have found that Dreams also captivate most women. Until recently, the feminine version of the Dream would have centered upon marriage, homemaking, and motherhood. For many it still does. Today, for an increasing number of women, the Dream may be the same as it has usually been for men: a career in the marketplace. This enlargement of the scope of feminine Dreams will have a drastic, difficult-to-calculate effect upon our society.

I want to add almost in a parenthetical sense that many "Dreamless" people exist. The reasons for this are many. Some young people never dreamed Dreams because their parents belittled them or short-circuited Dreams about the future because they wouldn't let go of their children. Dreams can become deflated through tragic events such as chronic illness, the premature death of a loved one that requires changes in one's vocational or educational plans, or even the random or unexpected events in the process of life that eclipse the Dream and make it necessary to pursue more expedient alternatives. A large number of people never really dream full Dreams about their own personal vocational development because their goals are too short-term. They get jobs to pay for expensive automobiles or to get married. They think about the present, not about the future. In such cases, little room remains for a Dream to take over and push.

But for the person who originally nursed a full-orbed Dream and for the person who never owned a Dream, during a period at mid-life the spiritual implications of all of this begin to emerge. The scrutiny of whatever the Dream has been and what it is becoming will arise, because one becomes aware of the passage of time, the shortness of life, and the gnawing question of accountability.

And what possibilities show up as people pass through the vocational drama of mid-life? Some finally face the fact that their Dream never got off the ground. Others conclude that the original Dream to which they committed their lives was a terrible miscalculation, an unfortunate mistake. And another group becomes painfully aware of crucial mistakes made through earlier adulthood years, which will make a good Dream virtually unobtainable and force them to settle for lesser achievements. Then some at mid-life find their Dream, once very general and probably too idealistic, achieves sharper focus and comes closer to being realized.

We must expect these kinds of questions and answers surfacing at mid-life; they should not alarm us. The exercise of the affair of the spirit may provide us with a major opportunity for a change or a midcourse maneuver or for an affirmation that we chose the right course.

I think I see a Dream emerging in the life of Moses when the Bible says that he went out one day and became aware of "the burdens of his people." This simple statement charts the growing sensitivity in this man's heart that something had to be done to relieve the oppression his own race lived under. As a young man, his pursuit of the Dream went awry. He resorted, through his enthusiasm, to anger at the flagrant injustice of an Egyptian overseer and killed him. So Moses had to leave town quickly, like a fugitive hopping an overnight freight train. It took almost four decades for God to revive the original Dream within him and mellow Moses to a point where he would achieve the specifications of the Dream according to God's way of doing things. Moses stood at the middle of his life when this reevaluation of things happened, and when he came through it, he was ready to begin the last third of his life with respect for the Dream and the direction it would lead.

In contrast, Israel later had a king by the name of Saul who had a Dream to become an effective king. But somewhere in the middle of his life, his Dream began to sour as he became paranoid about a man in the younger generation—David—who seemed to threaten his security. Saul's feelings of uneasiness were not relieved when he heard the latest hit tune being sung in the streets, "Saul has slain his thousands; David has slain his ten thousands." We don't know how the melody went, but the words devastated Saul.

Totally controlled by his Dream, Saul slowly lost his perspective, and when he tragically died later in mid-life, he had turned into a total failure.

This vocational drama will be quite real to anyone who values his or her existence. A woman who at mid-life has just lost all of her children to college, marriage, and their own vocations faces despair from loss of vocation. It strikes the man or woman who suddenly realizes that a new and younger generation is just behind (like David) and threatening to move more forcefully, at a greater speed. The drama happens to the person who at mid-life has reached all of his or her goals and suddenly wonders what it's all worth. Such a drama may cause the person at mid-life to wrestle with boredom, nonproductivity, or a wild inner urge to throw caution to the winds and make a major change in vocation.

But in a more subtle sense, the drama is most significant to the person who at mid-life looks at what he's doing and, having thought it all through, says, "It's just a job." That man has my pity.

Our vocational affair of the spirit passes through three stations. First, we make some unique mid-life discoveries about the things we're doing. Second, we begin to define how we feel about what we've discovered. Finally, we usually take some sort of action in response to our discoveries and our feelings. When that action has been taken, the vocational drama of high noon has come to its conclusion. Hopefully we take from the drama a view of our doing that makes it more than "just a job."

7

"I Don't Want to Be a Prostitute Anymore"

I visit with a young man with several years ahead of him before he reaches the inception of mid-life. Yet as our conversation unravels, I begin to sense that my friend has made some vocational discoveries normally reserved for men and women well into their middle years. It should have hit me, I think as we talk, that his job ages him much more swiftly than the jobs most people undertake. In fact the public speaks of retirement in his vocation when a man reaches his mid-thirties. A professional football player, he decided to quit the team several years before he really has to.

"What's causing you to hang it all up?" I asked him.

I'm not totally prepared for the frankness or even the vividness of his metaphor when he answers, "I'll tell you why I'm quitting. I have come to the conclusion that being a football player in the National Football League is just like being a male prostitute."

"A what?" I ask now that I'm at the edge of my chair.

"You heard me," he says. "I've decided that I'm nothing more than an athletic prostitute. Some businessmen pay for the use of my body on a football field. They make money off me. They'll use my body as long as I'm capable of getting it out on the field each Sunday and making it perform. But when I get hurt badly enough or get too old to perform better than some-body else, they'll pay me off and get a replacement. That's prostitution, from my perspective, and I don't want to be a prostitute anymore."

It is not necessary to determine whether or not anyone agrees with my friend's appraisal of a professional athlete's vo-cational character. But note that a man has evaluated his job in terms of an affair of the spirit, and he has concluded that on that basis his job lacks some elements which are now impor-tant to him. Having made a reappraisal of his vocation, he de-cides to quit.

My partner in this conversation agrees that he has not al-ways looked at football playing in such a unique way. "Good grief, no!" he says when I ask him if he's always questioned his role.

"When I first started playing football, it was plain, pure fun. I was bigger than most of my friends, and I had good coordina-tion. It was a natural thing for me to do. I loved every minute I was in pads. I made great friendships, received much recogni-tion, and learned a lot about people. I used to feel lucky to be a football player in college and in the pro leagues. But now my values and my perspectives have changed. This feeling about prostitution is something new. Now that I've had my experi-ences with the glamour, the winning, and the accomplishment of it all, I'm beginning to see some things in a different light."

No conversation I have ever had more appropriately illus-trated for me what I mean when I say that in the mid-life drama of vocation, we are apt to make some disquieting *or* sat-isfying discoveries about what we have been doing with our lives. Discoveries that may cause change (like my friend the football player); discoveries that may cause a realignment of priorities; discoveries that may cause us to work harder, or less, or for different reasons. We make them when we appraise our vocation from the perspective of what Saint Paul called "the inner person."

I cannot suggest, much less dogmatically assert, why people experience new discoveries about the nature of their vocations on the spirit level when they reach life's center point. Perhaps we could attribute it to one or a combination of many personal causes. Perhaps there simply exists an increasing sensitivity to the fact that one's allotted time for living and doing begins to appear less abundant than earlier days, when it seemed virtually inexhaustible. Or one begins to realize that energy, once easily renewable, no longer remains an unlimited reserve. Rather, we must carefully husband it, lest it be in short supply.

Then again the mystique of the middle years may cause us to question the worth of our personal contribution to the world in which we live. *What difference do I as a person make?* we each begin to ask ourselves. We seem strangely driven to make measurements of our doing. James Baldwin muses upon this same matter:

> Though we would like to live without regrets, and sometimes proudly insist that we have none, this is not really possible, if only because we are mortal. When more time stretches behind than stretches before one, *some assessments, however reluctantly and incompletely, begin to be made.* Between what one wishes to become and what one has become there is a momentous gap, which will now never be closed. And this gap seems to operate as one's final margin, one's last opportunity, for creation. And between the self as it is and the self as one sees it, there is also a distance, even harder to gauge. *Some of us are compelled, around the middle of our lives, to make a study of this baffling geography, less in the hope of conquering these distances than in the determination that the distance shall not become any greater.*

The discoveries I'm thinking about are, as I've said, affairs of the spirit. In other words they are spiritual evaluations made from a spiritual perspective. They do not come normally as a bolt of lightning; they accumulate—the result of a series of conscious and unconscious impressions and convictions that create a growing tide of mid-life mood and measurement. We come to new and sometimes frightening conclusions about ourselves and that which we do. But these come only when one can see beyond the surface: the glamour of touchdowns, the winning of games, and the signing of multiyear contracts. They come when someone asks, "Why am I here? Do I like what I see? Is what I am doing worth the cost?"

Discoveries? What kind? And in what categories? The people I've been listening to and the thoughts that have generated in my own mid-life spirit lead me to suggest several possible areas where people come to surprising discoveries about their own vocations.

A prime discovery happens, for example, when a person begins to find him or herself making frequent measurements of original vocational goals and objectives against *a new set of values and needs* that one seems to formulate during middle years. The discovery may not be a happy one if a clash exists between the ambitions of the twenties and the needs and concerns of the forties.

A man chooses, during the ambitious years of young adulthood, a vocation that demands enormous mobility in terms of frequent shifts of residence and extended periods of travel. In the early years, he finds little trouble in leaving a wife and a couple of small children behind. The excitement and the achievements more than compensate for the separations. But fifteen years into the vocation, something changes. There begins to emerge from within the inner self a hunger for certain stable and enduring relationships that could come only from a consistent home and family life. Such a *relational need* begins to ascend to equal importance with earlier vocational desires. If such a thing happens at all, it will probably happen in early middle years.

This man's discovery? That there is an aching conflict between a chosen pattern of vocation that keeps him on the road when a new emergent pattern of value calls upon him to establish a place to come to and persons with whom to have deeper relationships. In this case he finds the discovery discomforting. It demands radical readjustment of activities or values. And until the adjustment is faced and implemented (assuming it will be the correct one), he will experience much frustration and probably a tendency toward reduced effectiveness in all areas of life.

A quick survey of vocational values in early adulthood might be helpful, so that we can note the potential clashes with such mid-life needs. A typical early adulthood vocational value would be that of professional advancement or the acquisition of power within a chosen vocational system. We're talking about the old push to "get ahead and make something of yourself."

A second young-adult goal may simply be that of enlarging one's income potential and level of purchasing power. That's a pleasant way of saying that many people work simply for financial benefits. Surveys usually show that most workers do not see money as a central goal, but as a young adult value, it tends to appear regularly as one of the top factors of attraction to a particular vocation. Money purchases "freedom," opportunity, acceptance, and something called the "good life." Our American culture teaches many people to think that way.

Some as young adults started off with the design in mind of making a significant contribution to their world. I hear young people say, "I want to do something that will make a difference in the lives of people. I believe that the system needs to be changed; I want to be in a position to contribute to the making of those changes." Certainly a noble pursuit.

Rightly or (more often) wrongly, the earlier idealism slowly dissipates from the sheer force of practical needs, which by mid-life have risen to a preoccupying level of attention. Children's college expenses, dental bills, roof repairs tend to squelch a lot of earlier idealistic motivations. It becomes a classic pattern of clash as one set of values is exchanged for another.

Achievement can also be a young-adult objective. One pursues a graduate degree or professional certification and acceptance of some sort and then sets out to gain a stamp of recognition from peers or as measured by certain criteria of success within one's system of vocation. Simply to achieve the given level is enough. Money in this case may make little, if any, difference. A violinist sets out to be first chair in a symphony; a salesperson seeks to be a territorial sales manager; an assistant professor dreams of becoming a full professor and noted authority in a certain field; a laborer is ambitious to own his or her business.

Most young adult objectives rarely take into consideration factors in life that may be out of one's control. Young-adult ambition usually assumes unfailing health, supportive relationships, a system with little or no opposition, competition, or intersystem politics. Young adults usually assume that their world eagerly anticipates the arrival of a "messianic" individual, but they often face unanticipated roadblocks and pitfalls.

In the early sixties, for example, the American scientific community put a premium on the space program—launching satellites, putting a man on the moon, getting caught up with the Russians in rocket technology. Universities trained thousands of men and women as engineers to participate in the incredible effort that resulted in our successful moon landing in 1969. It seemed as if there were no end to the opportunities for anyone who entered the world of electronics, rocket propulsion, and the allied aerospace industries.

Few of the young adults who jumped on this bandwagon, settled down in expensive homes, and carved out exciting jobs realized how adversely they would be affected when President Nixon flew to Moscow in 1970 and signed the SALT I agreement with the Soviets. Few saw that the landing of the first men on the moon actually signaled a sudden reversal in the fortunes of the space industry. The landings meant that the great goal had been achieved and that many programs and personalities could be mothballed.

With the signing of SALT and the landing of a few men on the moon, large areas of industry suddenly went out of business as the government scrapped programs no longer needed for defense or research. Engineers were laid off by the thousands. Many lost the prestige and prerequisites that went with once absorbing jobs: parking spaces, secretaries, large salaries, promises of advancement. Men with doctorates in exotic disciplines of science found that they had less chance of finding a job than a man who had spent his life pushing a broom. No one foresaw this in the flush of young-adult ambitions. An original goal—all-consuming—had now betrayed them.

A second illustration of misconstrued priorities and values came to me in my office one afternoon when a father called on me to ask how he could reestablish contact with his fourteen-year-old boy. "I can't say that I know him very well," he admitted. "Frankly it's my fault; I spent six years working on an M.A. and the Ph.D., then I landed a tough job with my corporation. It demanded all my time. There was good money involved. So now we have a cabin on the Cape, a boat, and everything we need, but my kid isn't interested in going there; he isn't interested in spending time with me or his family. He says he just wants to be with his friends. I can't get to first base with him."

In both cases one's original objective did not conform to certain values or realities that emerged at mid-life. Some space engineers threw themselves into tasks that quickly became obsolete or useless to a changing society and *its* priorities. A father didn't understand that his relationship to his son would take on equal importance to the success he had once craved on his job. For the professionals in the space program and the man who had no contact with his son, the discoveries were painful.

A recent television commercial became a symbol of the second discovery about vocation that I often see mid-lifers facing. A rubbery-faced man leers into the camera while he holds up a cigar. He confidently predicts, "One of these days, sooner or later, we're gonna git—cha. Yup! We're gonna git—cha!" It's his way of telling the TV watcher that sooner or later he'll become addicted to the taste of these cigars.

It is a mid-life experience to suddenly come to the conclusion (or discovery) that our vocations, in one way or another, have "gotten us" or that they are just about to get us. My more dignified term for "being gotten" is *vocational entrapment.* When we decide that we cannot extricate ourselves from what we've been doing and pursue alternative vocations, we have sprung the trap. No one form of entrapment exists. I describe the condition which can arise because we cannot change our way of thinking, our way of doing things, our need for acceptance or a style and standard of living.

When Arthur Miller wrote *Death of a Salesman* he told the tale of vocationally trapped traveling salesman Willy Loman. A large part of his sense of entrapment in life came as a result of his job. Loman felt tired, beaten, and bored. On the surface he would have loved a change, but he had entrenched himself within a job and a mental attitude from which there was no escape. When he dared to approach a new and younger boss to ask for a promotion or at least a shift to the home office, he was refused and finally fired. Miller's title for his play *The* Death *of a Salesman* sets one to wondering when the death really took place. Wasn't Willy Loman really dead the day he discovered himself trapped at mid-life, imprisoned in a system partly of his own making? The story carries a lot of warnings about life, but perhaps one of the most poignant of the warnings is that of what a vocation can do to a man if he allows it to happen.

Vocational entrapment can be financial. A man earns a substantial salary as a broker of stocks and bonds. As the years pass, his family moves into a luxurious home, drives costly automobiles, and sends children off to expensive colleges. But in the middle of this onward and upward financial process, the man finds himself becoming slowly disenchanted with his vocation. One day we sit in his office, where a desk holds a console phone, a TVlike screen on which flash the stock transactions from the "big board," and the keyboard terminal that ties him directly to a Wall Street computer. I'm impressed with the atmosphere, but I soon discover that he feels depressed by it.

"I have come to the point where I hate going to work. I like this business less and less. There are just too many times when I find myself participating in other people's decisions and not feeling like I'm being entirely honest with the situation. There are simply too many opportunities to cross the line into a subtle kind of dishonesty where you're working on commission with other people's money. I'd really like to get out."

"Then why don't you?" I ask.

"I can't," he responds. "I'm between a rock and a hard place. I can't afford to quit. I could never make this much money at anything else. We've got so many bills at home that I'll have to keep on working at this income level. A change in jobs would mean an enormous financial step backward. We're in no position to face that."

The man in the impressive office discovers that he hates the place where he works, the things he does, and the person he sees himself becoming. But he lacks the courage to change, and it's partially due to the fact that he feels trapped. The job seems to have bought his soul, and he can't afford to buy it back. It will take a massive dose of strength to break the pattern at mid-life. His discovery—an affair of his spirit—is also not a pleasant one.

Vocational entrapment can also be an emotional experience. Some people may discover at mid-life that they need a job for their own emotional well-being more than the job needs them. I have noted for example, that many pastors find it difficult to be pleased with any other kind of a job if they have enjoyed being a leader among people for a number of years. Slowly they acquire a need for the applause, the affection, the attention given to someone who practices the healing arts of the spirit.

One such ex-pastor says to me, when I ask him if he's happy, "No, I can't say I'm as happy as I thought I was going to be. I had been looking forward to getting out from under the pressurized life, but now I find that I can't stop thinking like a pastor. Somehow, I keep feeling that what I'm doing now is second class in comparison to what I was doing when I preached each Sunday, called on people, and ran a church. I guess I spent too many years thinking like a pastor. Now I don't know how to think like someone else."

A woman who has chosen the vocation of a mother can experience this kind of entrapment at mid-life when her children leave home to enter adulthood. Many women have been taught that the glory of womanhood emerges in the privilege of motherhood. Thus motherhood as a vocation becomes a consuming dream for many young-adult women.

But can't that dream end in a nightmare if a woman is not prepared for the abrupt conclusion to that vocation somewhere in the mid-life period? A kind of emotional entrapment may occur if a woman allows her "job" to consume her so that all other activities in her adult life pale in contrast.

Morton Hunt, in a rather morose description of the woman who is emotionally entrapped from a vocation as mother, describes difficult moments:

> When the house is quiet and the children's beds never need to be made, now in the time of the empty nest she begins like a wounded bird to flutter about pitifully and aimlessly, all the more wildly if she invested all of herself in motherhood, derived none of the meaning of her life from other functions, and made no preparation for the second half of her life.

I have recorded in one of my notebooks the comments of a woman who describes her own sense of entrapment in this way: "I've just turned forty-three, I know what entrapment is all about. I've been a mother so long that now I don't know what I am as a person. My life is all at loose ends. I'm looking for something new to do, and the worst thing about it all is that I don't have the slightest idea of what it might be. It's hard to think of myself as anything but a mother."

The *Boston Globe* carries a sardonic essay by Rosemarie Mitchell, entitled "Her Agony at Being Thirty-Eight . . . With No Place to Go." Mrs. Mitchell writes of her feeling of entrapment, "There was a pain inside of me that wouldn't go away. Actually, it was more of an ache, an ache that comes with being 38 years old, a mother, a housewife, a nobody."

Mitchell goes on to explain her feelings:

> I told myself when all the children were in school that I'd do something, go back to teaching, or writing, to be someone of value and importance. But, in reality, *I never believed that day would come.* I would always be young and pretty, with a toddler running about, reminding me that I was, most of the time, happily tied down. It was true that I frequently envy Tom's freedom: out the door, briefcase in hand, the constantly changing world. But someday, I thought, they'll all be in school and I'll be free.

Perhaps you can spot the seeds of thought that frequently generate the bitterness and anger which have given birth to some parts of the modern women's liberation movement. Obviously, Rosemarie Mitchell senses some sort of betrayal by a vocation she'd eagerly entered when a young adult woman. She reveals even more as the article unfolds.

When approached by another woman and asked, "What do you do?" Mrs. Mitchell relates:

> I froze. I searched for impressive words, but there were none. "I'm home, this is the first year the children are all in school" hastily I added, "but I plan to work. At what? Well, I don't know yet . . . !"

Then later in her conclusion:

> And so the ache remains inside me. I read the want
> ads. I fiddle with the prospects of returning to school.
> I talk to acquaintances who shake their heads and
> agree the real estate business is tough. I listen to
> friends who've taken several courses over the years
> and now have jobs. My friends . . . the same ones who
> bragged about their devotion to their family, and how
> they'd never leave their children, but now they all
> have a place to go and I don't.

Mrs. Mitchell's comments may be unsettling. She may even
upset some of us. But if you hear nothing else, listen to her
anger. She has discovered herself trapped in a strange sort of
webbing that is part emotional, cultural, and relational and it
causes her psychic pain. She feels as if someone has hung a
sign on her that says OBSOLETE. It was at the beginning of mid-
life that she made her terrible discovery.

In quoting Rosemarie Mitchell I mean no negative commentary on the value and significance of motherhood, but I do
wish to highlight the anguish that can surface at mid-life if a
woman is unprepared and if, indeed, she has created a style of
life in which she becomes vocationally entrapped. We cannot
blame motherhood, but Rosemarie Mitchell failed to prepare
for her mid-life discovery and others did not challenge her to
do so.

Most men would not relate as intensely to the feelings of entrapment. But they would agree that fifteen or twenty years
within a single vocation often so affects one's way of thinking.
Truly it becomes almost impossible to think of doing anything
else. In this case a mind seems to have stiffened; it cannot select
other options as it once did and this, like some of the others, is
not a happy discovery.

At mid-life the majority of us will discover a third reality
about our vocational experience: *limits!* That there probably

exist vocational "altitudes" beyond which we can no longer climb in terms of success and position; that there are things we just can't do, positions and opportunities we probably won't be able to enjoy, and important people within our vocational sphere we will never meet.

I think I may safely say that virtually everyone learns something about personal limits at mid-life. And several different kinds of discoveries about limits could conceivably emerge. For example, some unexpectedly discover that they are far *less* limited than they originally thought. I think of a woman who once perceived herself as being bereft of any creative talent. Coaxed into an art class, she uncovered at mid-life a marvelous artistic gift. Her paintings now sell for several hundred dollars, and she gathers a crowd from the community whenever an exhibition of her work is announced. She discovered an expanded limit.

All too frequently many discover that their mid-life achievements cannot always match young-adult ambitions. Most people attach this depressing reality to the mid-life experience. The picture of the middle-aged man who becomes aware that he is being passed by for promotions, that younger people in the firm are making faster strides, that there exist new vistas in the state of the art of his chosen expertise that he simply cannot master. The upward path of his career has suddenly flattened. Of this moment Daniel Levinson writes:

> Often, a man who has worked hard during his 30's comes to recognize in the midlife transition that his accumulated achievements and skills do not provide a basis for further advancement. He cannot become a writer, educator, political leader or violin maker of the calibre he imagined. He will never rise to the level he sought in the military, the corporation, or the church. He will fall far short of his early dream. This is a crucial turning point. He may decide to continue in his present job, doing work that is increasingly

routine and humiliating. He may change to another job or another occupation, that offers more challenge and satisfaction or he may reduce his interest in work, performing well enough to keep employed but investing himself in other aspects of life such as family or leisure.

This experience, misunderstood or mishandled, can lead to a sense of panic, depression, or desperate and ill-advised behavior patterns. Native ability and hard work are traded for playing politics and undermining competitors so that one can maintain the valued status quo. When this happens someone cannot face limits—his own.

Joseph Heller's novel *Something Happened* amply describes a mid-life man's inner frustrations with his vocation. At one point the story's central character describes his relationship with a working associate—Jack Green.

> Often I protect and defend him when he is late or forgetful with work of his own, and I frequently give him credit for good work from my department that he does not deserve. But I never tell him I do this; and I never let him know when I hear anything favorable about him. I enjoy seeing Green apprehensive. I'm pleased he distrusts me (it does wonders for my self-esteem) and I do no more than necessary to reassure him. And I am the best friend he has here.

Something within our Western culture provokes us all to believe that limits are unacceptable. We tend to choose as our heroes those who seem to have no limits or those who have transcended their limits through brilliance, strength, or natural ability. Such are the ideal persons, and we nurse the notion, therefore, that we also should have no limits.

David, Israel's greatest king, grew up experiencing so many extraordinary victories and accomplishments that we find it hard to believe that he had any limits at all. It's fair to observe that he was used to acquiring or winning anything he wanted. But among his own personal objectives was the construction of an enormous temple in the city of Jerusalem. As he expanded the idea into a consuming ambition, there seemed no reason to believe that he wouldn't accomplish this project and place it alongside all the others, which had begun with the killing of Goliath.

But God had other ideas, and when it came to temple building, David faced a heaven-imposed limit. This part of his life-long ambition was simply not going to be satisfied. God had said, "NO!" The temple project would belong to David's son, Solomon.

The Bible records no evidence of David's bitterness over this limit. He seems to have accepted it realistically. He also seems determined that if this was his personal limit he would have to assist those who, with Solomon, would do the job in his stead. David spent his later days gathering materials and data necessary for the actual job. In accepting his own limit, David made it possible for someone else to get the job done (1 Chronicles 22). He's a positive example of a man who came to grips with a limit, accepted it, and rejoiced in someone else's opportunity.

A final vocational discovery that most frequently marks the middle years of our lives is very hard to pin down to a few words. I'll borrow a theologian's term and suggest that there comes a point in our vocational lives when we "demythologize" our careers. Put another way, we begin to see our "doing" in terms of real actions and achievements rather than in the glamorous perspective with which most of us began our younger years.

As a young pastor I drooled over the opportunities to lead a large congregation, to travel, and speak at various conferences, and to write for various periodicals and to author a book. Now some fifteen years later, while I love my job and the opportunities it affords, I have gone through a process of vocational demythologizing. I see the job I do in the more accurate dimensions of its fatigue, its responsibility, the mental and emotional drain it causes. In fact, like many others, I even feel tempted on certain occasions to have an attack of reverse ambition, namely to get lost in the pipe dream that one could go back to simpler days, when it wasn't necessary to face so many decisions, people, and responsibilities. In short, I no longer see my job as glamorous.

Preaching no longer seems an ego trip, but an extraordinary responsibility. Traveling is not an exciting activity, but a taxing necessity. Pastoring a large congregation doesn't really hold prestige; it's draining and often leaves one gasping at the end of the day for enough energy (mental and physical) to make it to bedtime. I'd like to keep my job, but its surface excitement won't dazzle me.

The unprepared mid-lifer finds the demythologizing of a vocation an upsetting experience. It means that some fall into a paralyzing boredom about vocation. For others, it results in frequent changes (every few years) as they seek a kind of perpetual glamour and excitement that simply aren't going to happen. Conversely, a healthy experience of demythologizing has occurred when one experiences excitement in living amidst a daily routine, in not running from a growing host of relational responsibilities that go with a growing vocation.

A few years ago I found myself seated next to a well-known television personality on a transatlantic flight. For almost five hours we talked about some of the salient issues of life. My traveling partner had no hesitation in admitting that he was a bored, unhappy man, feeling betrayed that success had brought him so little of that feeling of excitement he'd expected when he'd started. Looking back on our conversation, I now realize that at mid-life he was still tyrannized by the thought that, given enough success, his job would become one long orgy of excitement and satisfaction. I remember saying to him, "You know, you already have the three things the average American male thinks epitomizes vocational success: a beautiful young wife, more money from your work than you can ever spend, and a name so popular that in two lifetimes you can't handle all the invitations you get."

The memory of what my friend on the plane said has stuck with me. "You're right; I've got all that. But it's those very things that have conspired to make me generally miserable. For you see now that I have achieved them, I know—unlike those still reaching for them—that they're not worth having, not worth working as hard for as I've done. At least those who are still reaching have satisfaction in pushing for some sort of unknown but I'm already there, and I know that all I've done doesn't amount to anything. *I don't even have the fun of hoping anymore.*"

I think my friend told me that the day he demythologized his job, he couldn't face the conclusions. For him, it was not a pleasant experience.

Not everyone makes these same four discoveries I've outlined. Some, knowing and mastering these realities all along, had nothing to discover. Others will march all the way through life with circumstances and opportunities that make it unnecessary ever to face these discoveries. But among the majority of us who at mid-life face a combination of these discoveries, the effect can be devastating or delightful, imprisoning or freeing. And out of the discoveries we make about our vocations will come some inner feelings and decisions that will determine a large part of where our future takes us.

Section IV

Reflections on Mid-Life Relationships

8
Cutting Loose

If we could take a candid camera into a number of homes on any given evening, we might expose variations of the following relational themes.

The Johansons sit at a kitchen table scattered with the dirty dishes of supper. From other parts of the home come the noises of children already caught up in the activities of the evening. Husband and wife, Ken and Marjorie, sit in what appears to be a shocked silence, every once in a while rearranging silverware, glasses, or plates in front of them as if the action could justify the time spent sitting there actually doing nothing—except thinking.

The Johansons quietly assess the results of a conversation with their oldest son, Kirk, who at the age of seventeen is in his senior year at high school. Somewhere between the passing of the pork chops and the finishing of the diced carrots, he informed his parents that he does not plan to go to college next year. What he really wants to do, he's told his parents, is to "knock off from school for a year or two and travel. Get a job, maybe, and see what the world is all about." He goes on, "A couple of us are thinking about buying a van and heading out to California for a while."

Marjorie Johanson first swung into response to Kirk's announcements. His plans were unthinkable she'd said. His father had been working for several years, putting away money for Kirk's college education. Already they'd talked about various colleges and had even accumulated some catalogs. Why the sudden change? she asked. Didn't he have the sense to see that his parents were making possible something that other young people would give their right arms to have?

Kirk's father, Ken—given a moment to think by his wife's rejoinders—had pitched in, "Son, all of us would love to take a year off and go a lot of places, but there isn't time for that right now. Do that later on. You're young now; you've got few responsibilities or attachments. Press your education through. If you are to go on for graduate degrees, there may be as many as eight or nine years ahead of you. You can't waste time right now. Don't you want to make something out of your life? Why the sudden change?"

Conversation at the Johanson table degenerated from that point on. Kirk didn't really know why he wanted to take a van to California, but he did know that he'd lost interest in college. Did there always have to be a reason? he'd asked. Does life always have to be planned out to the tiniest detail? Is there only one way to live? What's so darned important about college, anyway?

It all conspired to make Marjorie flush with anger, and it pushed Ken into a frustration that finally ended in his saying to his son, "It's your life; if you want to make a fool of yourself and turn down every opportunity we've made available to you, go out and ruin it. Just remember this kind of conversation years from now, when you realize that you made a mess out of your own life." At that point Kirk had left the room.

That's why Ken and Marjorie sit there alone. Probably Marjorie's mind ranges from thoughts of how she'll explain Kirk's unorthodox behavior to her friends, to the unthinkable possibilities of her "baby boy" in the whirl of the culture of California.

Ken Johanson also thinks with swiftly changing impressions. He broods on the foolishness of wasting time, on how the boy is ever going to develop a career, on will we have to come and bail him out of trouble, and on why a tiny part of his innermost being actually envies his son's desire to break out of what is expected and to actually attempt something that Ken Johanson has wanted to do himself so many times: just leave schedule and responsibility behind. The conflicting thoughts confuse Ken, but he doesn't say anything about them, because he thinks Marjorie wouldn't understand. The chances are, however, that she would.

The Johanson home is not a comfortable place to visit tonight. This set a struggle between the generations in motion. No one knows where the lines are really drawn and that results in silence, hurt, betrayal, and sometimes, from a mother and father, even envy.

Down the street live the Stephen Doyles, married for ten years, both in their thirty-eighth years of living, enjoying their first home after several years in an apartment. A "late marriage" has caused these past ten years to be quite busy for Steve and Karen: establishing their own basis for relationship, the birth of two children, the pursuit of Steve's business, a partnership with a college roommate. Everything has been "today oriented" and they have had little time to think of tomorrow.

This evening Steve Doyle sits out on his patio alone. He would only reluctantly admit his feeling, since it's one of generalized fear, but two or three things have happened in the past week that have set off a sense of uneasiness within him. He would feel foolish if you asked him to put into words what makes him slightly morose or broodish this evening. Karen sensed it at supper and tried to increase the rate of conversation, but she failed. Now she's withdrawn and left him alone. What triggered Steve's depression?

Perhaps it began last weekend, when Steve and Karen visited their college campus for a ten-year reunion. They took a few minutes to drive across town, over to the first apartment they'd shared when they'd gotten married and Steve was in graduate school. *It would be fun,* they'd thought, *to see what the old place looks like.* "Let's go back and see where it all started," Steve had suggested.

At first they'd thought that they'd made the wrong turn when they got there, and they laughed about how much time had caused them to forget. But a few minutes later it hit them: They hadn't made a wrong turn. The apartment, the street on which it had been located, the whole block for that matter was gone! It no longer existed. It had all been purchased by the university and was now a large athletic field with a tennis court, a running track, and a practice baseball diamond for the school team. There was no trace that Steve and Karen Doyle had ever lived there. Some gigantic eraser seemed to remove their marital origins from the history books. Their first year of relationship no longer existed geographically. It bothered Steve somewhere down inside himself.

On Monday, when Steve returned to his office, a young man whom Steve had hired four years before asked if he could talk with him. After a few moments of conversational adjustment, the assistant, whom Steve considered a protégé, announced his plans to leave the firm. He was moving, he said, to Portland, where he would try his hand at doing the very things Steve had taught him.

Steve tried to protest that the idea was absurd. How could anyone think that he could get into business after only four years of exposure to it? The conversation ended with both men trying to cover up hard feelings. Steve gave him his best wishes, but he surprisedly discovered that he actually hoped that the "boy" would fail miserably, so that he could realize all he'd given up. *One thing is sure,* Steve pondered on Monday. *When he fails, I'm sure not going to take him back.*

The disappearing apartment and the resigning assistant had certainly been a blow, but they didn't compare with the impact a phone call had had on Steve Doyle this afternoon. The voice at the other end informed him that his business partner, a man just a year older than Steve, had suffered a mild heart attack in Atlanta, where he was on business. Recovery might take from six to eight weeks, and even then he'd have to slow down.

So what bothered Steve this evening on the patio? Was it only sorrow for his business partner? Perhaps. But anything more? Didn't Steve Doyle really have a feeling that his partner had let him down? In fact wasn't he failing Steve by having a heart attack? He not only caused Steve trouble, but he forcefully made him aware that people could have heart attacks at thirty-eight or thirty-nine. Furthermore, Steve's partner drove one more hostile message back at Steve: Like the apartment and the resignation earlier that week, things were changing at a tremendous rate around Steve, and he seemed unable to do anything about it.

The university had not contacted him to ask how he thought about ripping down the apartment (how absurd); his assistant had made the resignation decision without consulting him (but then why should he?); and now this stupid heart attack—it wasn't planned, it wasn't convenient, and it certainly didn't give one a sense of clarity about the direction of the future. *Why does a guy think this way?* Steve asked himself. He was mystified that there were no answers.

Not far from the residences of the Johansons and the Doyles live the Charles Kings. Frances, Charles's wife of eighteen years obviously feels upset, and Charles cannot seem to comfort her. She has spent the afternoon with her aged parents. During an unpleasant visit, Frances found her parents in an increasingly agitated condition. They accused her of not spending enough time with them and called her an ungrateful daughter. Further discussions revealed that they had made poor financial decisions. They were not eating well, not getting away from their home, and they complained about various aches and pains that previously seemed inconsequential to them. Things had fallen into a state of disrepair about their small house, and neither of Frances's parents seemed concerned. The only thing they were sure of was that they expected more attention from Frances.

Tonight Charles King's wife feels both upset and scared. She reminds one of Steve Doyle, who cannot explain the uneasiness he feels over his partner's heart attack. Does something within Frances almost resent the fact that her parents have grown too old to take care of themselves? What bothers her? that she might have to take care of them? No, that could be handled. Charles's income is adequate to pay for the needed care. It may lie in something else just a bit deeper however. Perhaps Frances senses that she no longer has parents.

Frances probably wouldn't put it that way, but that comes through her feelings. She is used to a lifetime of having had a strong father and a mother she admired. From early childhood she had cultivated the myth that her parents could do anything they wanted. Her father was a genius when it came to working with his hands. Her mother had kept an orderly house, a productive schedule, and a steadying influence upon all the affairs of the family. But none of this existed any longer. "Frankly, they seem like children," she reported to Charles. "They bicker, complain, are never satisfied, and seem plain self-centered."

Frances doesn't know it yet, but she's put her finger on the problem. Aging has turned her parents into "children." What may bother Frances is the one fact she doesn't want to acknowledge: Her childlike parents have exchanged roles with her. She now acts as the parent, and they take the place of the infants. That fact confronts Frances with responsibility, but it also does something more. It means for the first time in her life, that she plays the role of the strong one. Apart from Charles, no longer does anyone stronger than herself, to whom she can turn, exist in the family.

Before this year the quiet feeling remained that if anything went wrong (Charles's sudden death, bankruptcy, an overwhelming problem) she could turn to her parents. Now suddenly it was as if they weren't there. The "safety net" of forty-eight years had worn out and began to fall apart from the "rottenness" of a tragically aging reality.

It all hits Frances tonight. Since Charles had never been close to his parents, he cannot completely identify with Frances's inner struggle. He can only sit there and try to decode her spotty descriptions of her feelings. At best he can only see that they face a financial problem of how to take care of the folks until they die. It will be tight, Charles thinks, but he can manage it. A few extra sales each month will solve the problem. "So, Frances, don't worry about it," he says, "we'll take care of it," he goes on. But Charles doesn't understand that that isn't the problem. The absence of that "safety net" really confounds Frances; it's gone, and even Charles's money can't replace it.

Charles King works for a sales manager by the name of Willard Solomon. Willard Solomon and Patricia (he's always called her Trish) live in a better neighborhood because a large home was always important to Trish. Two children had come early in their twenty-four-year marriage, and now both were gone. The large home that Willard and Trish Solomon owned seemed like an empty mausoleum to Willard.

Trish put the home through at least three total redecorations, and even now she appeared to be talking about another job in the living room. When he'd come home the other night he found an interior decorator there, conferring with Trish. Willard hadn't liked it one bit, but at least it did keep his wife occupied, and it helped reduce the number of accusations she might level at him about whether or not he was an adequately attentive husband. Lately Willard Solomon found himself looking at his wife with some sense of disgust, when her back was turned. He no longer desired to touch her; he showed only marginal affection when they were in public and it appeared to be the respectable thing to do.

So their sexual life ceased to exist, and Willard subsequently blamed Trish's change of life, while Trish had blamed Willard's "silly fear" over periodic problems with impotence. Accusations replaced any mutual concern, and the marriage had come to a point where now sex was neither discussed nor ever attempted.

Perhaps that is why—when the Johansons, Doyles, and the Kings were at home that night—Willard Solomon had supper with one of the company file clerks at a little restaurant about fifteen miles out of town. Trish had planned an evening at the theater with several women friends. A day or two ago the women decided to attach dinner onto their evening plans, and Trish had told Willard not to expect her at home during the supper or evening hours. Willard casually responded that he'd probably catch up on work at the office, grab a hamburger when convenient, and get home later in the evening.

But in his mind thoughts were not that casual. For months Willard had found himself mentally preoccupied with a scenario of experience that might have been unthinkable in the earlier years of marriage. Thoughts focused on possible relationships with younger women whom he found attractive. He saw himself socially and sexually vigorous again, and each bout with fantasy lowered his resistance to the notion of actualizing his mental intentions.

Perhaps that's why, when Willard got up that morning, he chose to wear his best and youngest-looking suit to work. If Trish had been more sensitive, she'd have wondered why her husband left for a long working day looking as if he was heading for a gala ball. But her eyes had long since ceased trying to notice what her husband was doing or how he looked. Her own concern that day centered on appointments with an antique dealer, a wallpaper salesman, and a hair stylist, in preparation for the evening's big event.

And Willard? An hour after arriving at the office, he knew his plan for the evening. A young woman from the filing department had dropped by his desk several times already to deliver requested reports and other bits of data Willard thought were legitimately important. Then they enjoyed a bit more conversation in the coffee room at the mid-morning break. These encounters had been going on now for several weeks. The young woman, in her late twenties, was divorced, provocative in her dressing style, and aggressive in personality. Willard found it very hard to admit to himself that he frequently thought about her, creating in his mind various situations in which the two of them might spend time together. It seemed to Willard that during these daydreams he always felt much more complete as a person, much more the kind of person he actually saw himself as. The thought patterns made him feel as if he knew her a lot better than he really did.

So it was like a time bomb ticking away, waiting for the proper moment, and Willard Solomon now knew that today the moment for ignition had come. It took only some prolonged conversation over coffee and they had a date for the evening. It seemed incredibly easy. She would meet him near her apartment at 6:30. She needed, she said, a chance to break away, and she'd enjoy an opportunity to do something different.

Willard Solomon got very little accomplished that afternoon. Wasn't this the same feeling he'd had back in his teenage years, when he planned his first dates with girls? He'd arranged to have his company car thoroughly washed and cleaned out. He even slipped out and paid a ridiculous amount of money for a razor haircut and styling. When the workday ended, he shaved in the men's room, drenched himself with extra cologne, and with some amount of nervousness, headed toward the meeting place.

Willard's choice of restaurant had been deliberate, out of town, where the chances of being seen were strictly limited. Not far into the meal Willard found himself feeling freer than he'd felt for years. He laughed more, feeling more like the man he imagined himself to be, enjoying a sense of power and control that he'd not felt with a woman for a long time. Everything he said seemed to either impress or amuse the young woman across the table. He had not missed the fact that other men looked at her as they crossed the restaurant to their table. It all seemed so satisfying, so good. And it all made what Willard faced at home so stultifying and suffocating: his wife, Trish.

The stories of the Johansons, the Doyles, the Kings, and Solomons do not look attractive, but they are real. Despite their authenticity, they are not necessarily inevitable. The tensions, the feelings, the actions all exist because these four groups of adults were ambushed by forces and movements for which they were unprepared either in knowledge or spiritual moral resolve. Unprepared and uninformed, they caved in to depression, panic, and even wrong actions (which may have seemed right and good at least for a moment).

I think I understand where these four couples come from. I see their pressures in people with great frequency. I talk to them, and I listen to them attempt to describe what they think is the indescribable. Suddenly, they say, things are coming apart. Values—once unquestioned—seem up for grabs; attitudes—once unconscionable—handcuff a person; relationships—once thought to be unalterable—slip and slide toward unknown conclusions, and each finds it all very scary.

How could these four couples have been helped? Could they have faced these realities with greater grace and actually turned into positive experiences with growth and joy for all? I'd like to emphasize a most positive *yes*. The people involved in my tales were not taught, were not prepared, were not challenged to see that the potential relational stresses that face us in the years of mid-life can either provide obstacle or opportunity. They chose their reactions.

Don't we recognize stresses in every age? We teach children to avoid things that are hot, sharp, and poisonous. We instruct adolescents about their legal limits, the force of their sex drives, and the importance of building up disciplinary habits in the mind. We hopefully prepare the engaged adult for marriage, through counseling; for his or her career, through technical and graduate schools; and for child care, with books and courses. Then we stop! Somehow we assume that the compilation of all that knowledge will allow a middle adult to move ahead on his or her own and automatically decode the nuances of change that life constantly presents.

The basic reason for the panic in these four homes lies in unpreparedness. Unnamed feelings, frustrations without an apparent source, actions without an obvious logic—the stresses of the middle years move with freedom in the lives of many people because they have never been uncovered, defined, and thus defeated.

These four couples essentially dealt with relational struggles. They were not prepared for the fact that the mid-years seem to cover a period when everyone around changes in some significant way. The Johansons watched their oldest son struggle out of adolescence and into adulthood. They simply didn't like the direction of his efforts. The Doyles sensed change in themselves and in the associations around them. Someone left Steve Doyle, and a part of him resented it; another person weakened on him and caused a serious inconvenience, while reminding him that it could also happen to him. Frances King had for the first time been forced to confront the dramatic changes in her parents. Yes, she had known that they were growing old, but now for the first time she saw that aging can reduce people to the point where they can no longer play the role that Frances had so long come to depend upon. Trish and Willard Solomon apparently lost whatever marital happiness they had enjoyed when their children departed into adulthood. That left Trish with a beautiful but empty home, and Willard had a modestly successful career that seemed to go nowhere. Instead of looking toward each other, they looked away at mid-life: she to her house and other women friends (probably in the same predicament), Willard to another woman, who helped him reclaim for a moment the times when life seemed more exciting and promising. In each case people became engulfed by relational stresses they had not expected to face.

As human beings created in the image of God we are essentially relational. That is our most unique quality. Relationships among human beings provide far more than just a basis for mutual survival. Relationships enable us to grow toward the potential of our God-designed humanity. We grow because we encourage one another, because we affirm one another, because we rebuke one another; we support and defend one another. We provide one another with augmenting skills and capacities so that things get done in life that could not be done by one's doing or working at them alone. In its healthiest sense, these are all the acts of love. And we love one another in increasing amounts of intensity, the strongest love perhaps to be found in the marital and parental relationships.

Because the atmosphere of relationship forms an important part of our growth, our security, and our identity, we become instinctively sensitive whenever these relationships undergo any kind of change. The closer the relationship, the greater our sensitivity to anything that threatens it from within or without.

One of the great sins of humanity lies either in our failure to perceive the genius of relationship, thus failing to properly cultivate it, or in our taking various relationships for granted, thus missing the importance of maintaining and sustaining them. Often, either out of rebellion or ignorance, human beings will allow a number of things to get in between themselves and the relationships that are so crucial to spiritual and mental health. The pursuit of profits or prominence or the need to win or just plain self-centeredness, to name a few, can devastate relationships and leave us with consequences that will haunt us for an entire lifetime.

As I muse upon the dramas at the high noon of life it seems worthwhile to highlight the character of change in four relationships potentially significant to every one of us. In each of the four, the mid-life period is usually marked with a necessity of our saying a kind of "good-bye" as people intimate to us alter relationships by leaving us. Conversely, we may feel a sense of "hello" as other significant relationships take on a richer and deeper color for the rest of our lives.

The four that catch my interest concern: our children, if we have them; our aging parents; our close friends; and our marital partners. If risk exists in the venture of writing about these four it obviously lies in the sweeping generalizations necessary to cover the enormous diversity of possibilities that our relationships face during this time of life. For every observation one can cite a score of exceptions; for every principle a dozen mitigating circumstances remain. But because I see people wrestling with these issues on a daily basis, it seems worth the attempt to bring to the surface the relational matters that most often gain the attention of the man and woman at mid-life.

9
Letting Go

I think I understand Ken and Marjorie Johanson's mood as they sit dazed at their kitchen table. Haven't all of us known the frustration of conducting a conversation with someone we love and discovering that each appears to be dealing with a different system of logic?

The explosion in the Johanson home had not really come without warning. There had doubtless been other occasions, each increasingly confrontative, as Kirk's mother and father sensed their son beginning to put distance between himself and them, striking different and sometimes adverse positions in matters pertaining to values, behavior, and plans for the future. The two generations clashed over all sorts of differing perspectives.

In the heated discussion about the comparative merits of a year in California or a year at college, for example, Kirk's parents expressed concern about the matter of time use. To them there is less and less time, and any thought that their son, Kirk, might have of wasting a year of life confounds them. Time slips away, they reason; we may never reclaim it. Time is an expensive commodity. How can Kirk treat it so lightly? This perspective seems very clear to a man and woman who have put more than half their lives behind them.

But it isn't so clear to a seventeen-year-old boy. Rightly or wrongly, for Kirk the priority issues pivot on the pursuit of personal liberty, some general curiosity about the world, the desire for some "fun," and the question as to whether or not there exist viable alternatives to the achievement-oriented system of living taught in the Johanson family. In announcing his tentative plan, Kirk may simply be testing his parents to see how resistant they continue to be regarding his coming independence.

But his parents, Ken and Marjorie, who have invested heavily in the bringing up of their children, may also view things from the perspective of efficient and respectable performance, and they will feel tempted to grant independence only on their own grounds. Their way they think is "the way" that anyone who wants to amount to something does it.

Perhaps the memory of a discussion earlier in the week with a friend whose daughter has received a scholarship to a private university compounds Marjorie's attitudes. Then again, she thinks of her own sister's son, completing his premed schooling and anticipating a career in general surgery. In contrast to this, how can she seriously represent her own son's choice to sun and surf in California? Given her value system, she cannot. Thus her thoughts focus on a sense of what she thinks of as waste and the feeling that somewhere along the line she hasn't been the sort of mother her friend or her sister have managed to be.

The underlying issue in all this remains the matter of saying good-bye to Kirk. Not the good-bye that they might say if Kirk does indeed go through with his California fantasy, but rather the good-bye that occurs when child becomes adult, through the passageway of adolescence.

In my use of the word *good-bye* I do not suggest a termination of or a sense of finality in the parent-child relationship, but rather a recognition that an important change has taken place. The one saying farewell has assumed responsibility for his or her own life; control and accountability have shifted from parent to child. While relationship remains, it is now different, altered for the rest of everyone's life.

The good-bye said between parents and children often takes place as more of a gradual process than a point in time. How smooth the process becomes depends upon the parties involved, how prepared and equipped they are to accept it. Perhaps the first indications of the good-bye process emerge soon after the onset of puberty. In Kirk's life the farewell process occurred almost imperceptibly in early stages, here and there something like a bubble or two harmlessly rising to the surface of water and then seeming to disappear.

But the process began to accelerate, and now more and more decisions are being made and opinions expressed that suggest that Kirk Johanson is becoming more of a "Kirk" than a "Johanson." Part of the reason for the blowup in the kitchen lies in the fact that Ken and Marjorie have not become attuned to the signs of their son's good-bye. While they felt prepared to send him to a college dormitory, they were not ready for an alternative destination that was his choice, not theirs.

Not surprisingly as their first instinctive reaction when their son makes a measurable break from them, they ask, "Where did we go wrong?" It is really an unfair question, based on the assumption that somehow correct parental performance would result in Kirk accepting his mother's and father's opinions and judgments. This they appear to expect him to do, even without the advantage of learning lessons and accumulating the wisdom his parents think they have. Kirk, they reason, quite willingly sees life as they have seen it.

If that much misunderstanding exists between Kirk and his parents, the Johanson home will experience continual pain until Kirk indeed leaves. People within the kitchen that evening hear two different agenda. Parents say, *If you are that unwise, you're not ready to leave us;* and a son says, *I've got to leave if I'm ever going to become wise.* And when Kirk finally stomped out of the kitchen in rage, it was plain that no one had really heard the other.

Scripture frequently acknowledges the transition I have called the good-bye between parent and child. Boil down the passages on the subject of farewells in families, and you will discover that families release children to a new generation of life in one of three ways. The first was healthy and normal; the second and third were tragic and ugly.

Moses recognized that the healthiest good-bye occurs when a young man or woman leaves his father and mother and cleaves to his or her spouse. Leaving takes a special moment among the great events of life. It happens when a son or daughter is desirous, prepared, and equipped (at least marginally) to strike out on an independent passage of experience and thus depart from the luxury of parental protection and direction. Moses, of course, describes leaving from the perspective of marriage, and thus it seems a concept cast as a momentary act. But in fact, from a family perspective, the leaving has been in gradual motion for some time.

In my book *Magnificent Marriage,* I tried to show that leaving meant far more than vacating one bedroom in order to occupy another. Leaving, I suggested, has psychological, spiritual, economic, and geographical implications. Leaving means that an offspring assumes responsibility for him or herself. Apart from continuing general family fellowships, the son or daughter who leaves will not return. The only exception might occur in the event of a husband's death, where in certain cultures, the widow did return, for the purposes of support, to the domain of her father or other dominant family members.

In the biblical culture everyone left to get married sooner or later. Not necessarily so today. In twentieth-century Western culture we have created a special time of transition that we set aside for further education, and we call this adolescence. As a period of time, adolescence actually extends a bit beyond the teen years, if measured in terms of educational experience. During this time of education and training, teens progressively leave and may ultimately complete the good-bye even if marriage is not in the plans. One alternative can be the pursuit of a career and the single life. In some cases adult "children" actually return home because they cannot afford the high cost of establishing a home for themselves. And not a few return because independent entry into society is too abrupt and frightening.

But the principle of leaving remains the same in all of these cases. Leaving without a wedding ceremony may not be symbolized in the same official way, but it has similar implications for both the "leaver" and the "left." At that moment parents and children indeed part ways and drastically change a style of relationship that has substantially existed for eighteen to twenty-two years. In the best of all circumstances, this can be a moment of great drama, a bittersweet mixture of both joy and sadness.

Biblical writers saw children leaving their parents in a second way. This quite unattractive method I simply call rebellion. This is "leaving" in its extreme sense, and a strong sense of relational violence accompanies it. Rebellion in the family has its earliest roots in an untamed spirit; a sense of rejection enhances it, and an unreasonably repressive atmosphere may inflame it.

Under such circumstances an unavoidable good-bye must be said sooner or later, because all relationships within the family become affected and increasingly untenable. The father of the Prodigal Son would certainly have understood this, and it caused him to finally release his son to the consequences of his own choices. We may see this sort of extreme leaving in the Deuteronomy passage that provides for the execution of rebellious sons who will not accept authority. This frightening edict pointed out how delicate stable relationships become when rebellion continues.

To complete the concept of good-byes, one has to add to the principle of leaving and rebellion relational change by death. There is no way to pursue this tragic dimension of family transition except to recognize its reality. In one of these three ways, leaving, rebellion, or death, every normal child inevitably departs the home of his or her parents, and in the majority of cases for the parents this will happen in a mid-life experience.

How do we perform as mid-life parents under such circumstances—the best and the worst? The answer lies in our capacity to recognize and prepare for the process of leaving by learning to release our children to the life God has called them to.

The key word is *release*—letting go! In the best of all relationships, it is never done dispassionately. We do not sink our affection, our resources, our very lives into children only to wave good-bye without regret. As I pass through the early stages of this myself, with two growing adolescents, I sense my twin feelings of pride in their growing independence and sadness in the loss that relentlessly advances in my direction. I must constantly fight the urge to hold them closer, to do their thinking and believing for them as their choices in life become more and more significant in terms of long-range consequences. Perhaps what appears as a protective dimension of my life is really also a selfish side of my love for them. I know that I alone do not experience this, because in my pastoral role at weddings I see mothers and fathers of brides and grooms wiping away tears that obviously contain a mixture of joy and sorrow.

Resistance to release provides a sad alternative. Some of us witness the pathetic situation of a set of parents who have lost a child in death and who cannot seem to actually let the child go. They hold on to his or her memory by living in the past. They endlessly reason amongst themselves as to what might have happened if they had performed differently in the circumstances surrounding the death. Perhaps they attempt to maintain the child's bedroom exactly as it was the day of their loss. We see them struggle with various moods, such as bitterness, depression, and accusation. They often become jealous of other, more fortunate parents. If we love them, we attempt to cajole them into accepting their son or daughter's death, and we urge them to put the past behind and get on with the present and the future.

Such counsel does not ignore honest grief, for all of us will grieve at the good-byes of our children. Rather we plead for grief that eventuates in healthy release and transition for both the child and the parents.

I guess I recall the tragic picture of parents unable to release a dying child, simply because it becomes an extreme example of what many parents may do in a subtle way when they face the good-byes of children through the more normal channels. Stress and tension may exist on those occasions also, and the question remains: Are any of us ready for it?

A worried mother doesn't think her family is ready when she tells me, "My husband and our son were wrestling out in the living room the other night, laughing a lot and generally having a good time. They've done it a lot in the past, and I've grown used to it, although I'm always afraid they'll break something. But suddenly on this occasion a strange thing happened. The laughing stopped, and I could hear them grunting a lot and breathing hard. When I went in to see what was happening, it was obvious that they were very close to fighting. The wrestling match had grown serious. My son was close to getting the best of my husband, and I could tell that they were actually fighting with all their strength. My husband's face turned so red that I began to worry about him having a heart attack. I sensed that for some reason he couldn't afford to lose. When I finally began to scream at them to quit, my boy finally left the room with a kind of knowing laugh, but my husband took the thing very seriously. He sat in a chair for the longest time, just seeming to think about what had happened."

This mother has seen something that happens in different versions. She saw it in a wrestling match. I've seen it in my own family—most recently when my sixteen-year-old began to regularly destroy me in games of one-on-one in our backyard basketball court. I remember the evening I suddenly came to the realization that I could no longer relax and let him have the

lanes and the shots. Now he gets the shots and the lanes because he earns them. Today my only defense is to play dirty—
what son would ever call his father on that? It's the age-old fact
again: My son moves toward physical prime; I move away
from it. He enjoys reveling in it; I seek to repress it. When we
study the parental response to the mystery of leaving, each of
us needs to ponder something: A part of us—the Bible calls it
sin—tends to resist commitment when relationships begin. We
resist to the extent that commitment demands a dedication to
another person beyond a point of our own self-interest. Yet
another part of us—I think the Bible would still call it sin—reluctantly releases another person in a relationship when the
time has come.

This second relational dynamic—that of release—a mid-life
person finds most challenging when it comes time to say good-
bye to children. On the surface we may say, "When our children leave, we'll have more time, more money, fewer hassles."
But at a deeper level we may actually tend to subtly hold on,
postponing the release for a later or what we think of as a better time. Perhaps we should ask ourselves why that just might
be true.

Resistance to release might stem from a sense of guilt—real
guilt or false guilt. As we near that point where our children
begin to show the evidence of leaving our home, we may begin
to sense patterns within them that make us uncomfortably
aware of our ineffectiveness as parents, at least measured by
our own self-imposed expectations. Frequently on such occasions parents too frantically begin to play catch-up ball.

The pastoral team with which I work notes the enormous
rise in counseling appointments by disturbed mid-life parents
whose children have entered the age perimeters of fourteen to
seventeen. We rarely have anyone come to consult with us
about parental strategies and tactics before this period in the
lives of their offspring, unless a child has revealed seriously ab-
normal behavior characteristics.

When a pastor is approached by parents of adolescents, the

questions sound like this. "Would you talk with my son, John? He seems to have lost interest in spiritual things. I can't ever find out what he's thinking."

Another may say, "Our daughter doesn't ever want to be with the family; she's only interested in going out with her friends. We've planned a tremendous summer vacation that we thought she'd enjoy, and we can't believe now that she doesn't want to go."

Behind these well-intentioned concerns lies a growing awareness of potential failure. In our achievement-oriented way of life, the price paid for advance degrees, the rise up the career ladder, and the pursuit of respectability and security may be so intense that parents have mistakenly given minimal attention to everything else, including adequate intimacy with children. Thus when the process of leaving begins, a mother or father may suddenly become alerted to that which has been previously misunderstood or neglected. A policy of resistance may result: Let's slow down the leaving process a bit, it is reasoned, until we can correct any wrong patterns of parenting developed in the earlier years.

A second reason why some of us resist releasing our children to the leaving process is closely allied to the first. Now the behavior pattern reflects not so much our children's failure or even our sense of assumed failure, but rather a change in our mid-life values. It has been repeatedly observed that the onset of mid-life engenders a desire for deeper and broader qualities of relationships. This especially proves true for career men and women, and one of the first places where that quest shows itself is in the realization that we never got to know our children while they grew up.

More than one father has suddenly showered his time and attention upon an adolescent son or daughter and come away mystified by the response received, "Thanks, but no thanks." This parent may experience the temptation to purchase an adolescent's friendship through the acquisition of things he or she might seem to want quite badly, such as a motorcycle or a club membership (if indeed one has the money). A father suddenly invites his son or daughter to travel with him, work for him, to sit down and simply talk with him. Why? Because a need to know one's kids more intimately has abruptly made itself known. There may be the frustrating discovery that the desired intimacy is no longer possible. Now we may actually need our kids more than they need us. It seems a rule that what intimacy parents and teenagers enjoy was almost always cultivated before the age of twelve—and rarely after it. But in our headlong rush to achieve a formerly ignored knowledge of our growing children, we may desire to retard the normal leaving process, trying to buy time for ourselves.

Resistance toward leaving may stem from a third source, that of parental conviction. But until a child adheres to the family's definition of maturity, the parents are not ready for the leaving.

That's what may have been going on in the Johanson kitchen when Kirk expressed his intention to head toward California after high-school graduation. Marjorie and Ken Johanson want Kirk to mature through their teaching and personal precedent. It hasn't occurred to them so far that if Kirk is forced to find a job, confront a different culture, arrange for his own living logistics, and discovers the pitfalls of unprotected relationships, that he just might develop a concept of maturity quite similar to that of his parents.

In fact, Marjorie and Ken have more than once said to Kirk, "When you get out on your own, you're going to see that money doesn't grow on trees. You're not going to take your clothes, your meals, and your home for granted, because you'll be paying for it." Interesting that Kirk's parents, having warned about such a moment, now want to avoid it. Convinced of the negative potential of the California possibility in Kirk's life, they cannot face a positive result. It doesn't occur to them that if they release Kirk, some time may indeed be lost (a quarter or two of college), but their son may gain a level of maturity that he could never have achieved at home.

We resist the leaving of those most closely attached to us because we know more about them than anyone else does. Our familiarity with them makes us privy to their weaknesses and their blind spots. We presume failure rather than affirm the potential of success. This incidentally happens all too often amidst our most intimate relationships.

Finally, it is possible that mid-life parents feel tempted to resist the leaving of their children because it reminds them of their own seeming obsolescence. A son or daughter's leaving tells them in a way not so subtle, that they are not needed any longer.

For some mid-life women children have become the ground of their meaning to life. They have developed a need for the affection and response of offspring and find it almost an unbearable grief to say good-bye. Thus the unconscious tendency exists to hold on tightly, to resist a child's test of wings. In such a case everyone loses.

This can also occur if mid-life parents sense that children form the glue that holds their marriage together. The offspring may have been the center of marital attention and conversation. Parents never actually anticipated life "after leaving," and now that the last good-bye appears on the horizon they may experience panic, anxiety, or even anger at being left. All of us have seen the even sadder spectacle of the marriage held together only by the presence of children, which quickly dissolves as soon as they complete their leaving. It is indicative of this that a high percentage of marriages terminate at the twenty-fifth anniversary, in the early stages of mid-life.

None of these descriptions of parental predicament and performance attract one. In fact they seem shocking, almost unreal when placed on paper, and one wonders at the ignorance of adults, that they cannot notice these sorts of relational dynamics and realize they must halt them immediately. But I can only observe that such things do occur and with greater frequency than anyone imagines. With regularity I see them in the lives of families where parents are approaching the high-noon period of life unprepared for what awaits them. Little in the conversation that Kirk Johanson had with his parents really had to happen. Ken and Marjorie got ambushed and caught in what we call a no-win situation, because they weren't prepared. Had they understood the relational dynamics through which mid-life fathers and mothers and adolescents all pass—ironically, at the same time—the conversation in the kitchen could have concluded with a sense of dignity and affirmation all around.

So later, when I sit and visit with the Johansons, we review many of these things and talk about alternatives that may resolve an unsettled matter and help them understand how they got to this unanticipated place in their family life.

Ken Johanson likes to remember his son Kirk as a small boy: always obedient, happy, and easy to please. Ken tells me that he never anticipated any of those tensions he'd heard about in other homes in his as he saw them the other night. Kirk, he'd always thought, was special.

But now he faced those tensions, and as Ken sits visiting with me he admits that the distance between him and his son is largely his own fault. He worries out loud about where things are heading, both in his relationship to his son and his wife. The discussion about college and California had been an eye-opener to him. Suddenly he's come to realize that Kirk stands on the verge of making decisions that have lifelong implications, and Ken has not communicated about these with his son or his wife.

In this conversation I do not just act as a pastor and Ken as a person seeking pastoral counsel. More than that, we are both men with teenage children; we ourselves are the same age; and we share similar hopes for our families.

So our conversation moves in the direction of affirming the importance of accepting the differences that naturally occur between a father and his maturing son. Disagreements always will occur, we say to each other, about the things such as tastes in automobile models, clothing styles, and music. We agree that such differences do not necessarily signal that the son or daughter in a stable home environment is in a state of rebellion. Rather, they form part of a process in a family that makes each person as wonderfully different as a snowflake.

It follows, I tell Ken Johanson, that just as we prepare our kids to make their own choices, we have to prepare ourselves for the day when those choices are made—especially if a few of them surprise or even distress us.

"But wouldn't you feel disturbed," Ken interrupts, "if you saw your son throwing away a year at college simply to take off for the West Coast and an odd job or two?"

"Of course," I answer. "But that's because you and I've got twenty-five years to assess the results of the choice. Listen, assure me," I go on to challenge Ken, "that when you were eighteen, if you had the same opportunities kids have today, you wouldn't have turned your back on a chance to swing free for a short while and do some traveling."

Before assuring me, Ken thinks about it for a moment and then begins to grin. "It's funny that you mention it, because we often used to sit around and fantasize about going off to Europe and hitchhiking for a year."

"Why didn't you do it?" I ask.

"None of us had the money," Ken responds, and he and I both know that the case against Kirk's logic about California begins to grow thin. It makes sense to those of us who've had time enough to reap rewards and regrets, but even then we're not always sure.

As fathers, Ken Johanson and I have only two major things to give our children: Someone has labeled them roots and wings. In the first years of Kirk's life, Ken's parental agenda was that of roots. It was the time to build a family fence around his son, to give him the time to "root" himself in beliefs and values, in habit patterns and conduct that would clear the way for responsible adulthood.

But then a time came when Ken had to deliberately shove

Kirk from the nest for trial runs to test his growing wings. If Ken Johanson was wise, he would protect his son less and less from stress and error, so that Kirk could burn into his own spirit the mental and spiritual data that would allow him to become an increasingly mature person.

That's where the differences emerge, I suggest to Ken. We have to kick away the rules and regulations and trust that our kids have internalized it all for themselves. Then as they make their choices, we affirm the process by which they were made, assuming that the choices were good ones. And sometimes we have to allow them the freedom to make bad choices. That's where we mid-lifers often get into trouble. Having made bad choices occasionally ourselves in the past, we don't like to see our kids repeat them. It's part of the exercise of saying good-bye to them. At times we simply must remain quiet.

Ken looks back across the last few years with his boy. He acknowledges that their relationship frequently tested their relative strength. Kirk always tried to prove that he was a somebody, and Ken painfully admits, he attempted to prove that Kirk hadn't quite arrived yet. Rather than affirm Kirk's attempts at entering manhood, Ken tended to squelch them. Life in the Johanson home had become a chain of confrontations of the sort that led to a conversation like the one in their kitchen a few nights before. Ken and Marjorie's reaction to Kirk's proposition had been so inflexible that the boy finally walked out. Never again would they raise the subject.

As Ken unfolds his description of that fateful kitchen conversation, I wonder aloud if Kirk's anger had not been directed more at his father and mother's inability to at least give him the chance to talk through a decision than at their apparent lack of permission for him to implement it. Wasn't Kirk asking to do some adult thinking with his mother and father, while they did some youthful thinking with their son?

Saying good-bye to Kirk is going to be difficult, under the best of all circumstances. His leaving will produce a sharp change in the Johanson home and in the marriage. Are Ken and Marjorie prepared? The kitchen conversation suggests that they may have some catching up to do.

If Ken and Marjorie's marriage is weak, Kirk's eventual leaving either to school or California may drive a wedge further into their relationship. Ken may direct his energies more deeply into his work or the pursuit of a personal hobby. Marjorie may face a mild recession of inner spirit and then rebound with the announcement that she's going to get a job. And while there may be certainly nothing wrong with that intention, she may wish to do that simply to gain a measurement of her life's work in terms of money and acquisition of things. She might feel that a life of servanthood as a mother betrayed her.

As Kirk prepares to leave, this important matter surfaces: What can Ken and Marjorie Johanson do to smooth out the transition overtaking them? How can they cope with the change? A few attempted answers to that question emerge in a later meeting, when Marjorie joins her husband for a second visit.

First we talk about the spiritual level of this relational change. I want the two of them to realize that their marriage is complete before God, with or without Kirk. They made a commitment, I remind them, at the beginning of their marriage, to serve each other under all circumstances. All right, I suggest, Kirk's leaving is a circumstance of change. At this time their original commitment to each other in marriage ought to be renewed.

In our congregation we have occasionally included within a wedding ceremony something we call the celebration of parenthood. Early in the wedding the parents of both the bride and the groom leave their front-row seats, carry two lighted candles to a three-piece candelabra behind the altar, and light the two outside candles. In so doing they symbolize the years in which they have birthed and raised their children. After each of the couples have lit their candles, they join hands in a greeting, signaling their approval of the coming union between their offspring. The candles lit and the greetings given, they then take their seats. Later the bride and groom will take those candles and use them to light a center candle, thus completing the symbolism suggesting that what was once two has now become one flesh both in commitment and deed.

I have been very careful in every wedding where it could be done with integrity, to comment upon the fact that a ceremony of marriage exists not only for the bride and groom, but also for the parents, who terminate their essential responsibility for their children and release them to their new commitments. Where parents have raised godly children, I have done my best to commend them during a wedding ceremony, all the time helping everyone to recognize that a new relational state of affairs exists.

We aid ourselves in making adjustments, when good-byes are said, when we celebrate acts of completion and beginning. Even though releases occur, more often than not, as a process, it helps to recognize a particular moment when the good-bye becomes official or complete, and that is what a wedding ceremony is all about. In the case of a single son or daughter entering adulthood apart from marriage, it might not hurt for a family themselves to hold a celebration of sorts in which parents and son or daughter recognize a different state of relationship as now existent. In effect, our Jewish friends do this in part when they hold a bar mitzvah for a son or a bat mitzvah for a daughter and signal the emergence of that child into the period of adulthood.

I have often encouraged people like the Johansons to further mark the leaving of a son or daughter by planning a great event for themselves. A sort of mid-life honeymoon, which can be anticipated in the future. Some couples have saved for an extensive trip; others have made plans for the wife to return to college to pursue a once desired degree. Many creative ways exist in which to signal a new phase of life and then to anticipate it with excitement.

The process of saying good-bye to Kirk could also have been

enhanced if Ken and Marjorie Johanson had communicated more thoroughly in earlier years about the importance of letting their son make more of his own decisions.

Interestingly enough, both parent and teenager make the ultimate good-bye easier every time a parent urges a son or daughter to solve a problem alone. "Daddy," a daughter says, "can you fix my desk lamp? The switch won't work." If the girl is thirteen or fourteen, there's no reason why a father might not suggest that she learn how to do it herself. A son is being increasingly released if he is taught how to wash his own clothes, and it would not hurt for him to learn how to fix his own supper. I saw a noticeable difference in my fourteen-year-old daughter's self-confidence when she flew from Boston to meet me in Birmingham, Alabama, and had to change planes by herself in Atlanta. And my wife and I saw remarkable steps in the maturing process when we permitted our sixteen-year-old son to stay alone at home with an older friend, so that he could keep his summer job while we took a vacation.

Release takes place gradually in such events. For children, it means the building of confidence in their capacity to handle situations; parents take one more step in realizing that their offspring can get along without them and that they can even get along without the children. We will miss them, of course, and our home will seem empty when the final good-byes are said for college, jobs, or marriage. But life will not end. All of us who have done this will have tasted the good-byes bit by bit, and while they are bittersweet, we indeed find them palatable.

Our son, Mark, was barely ten when Gail and I began to think as best we could about what mid-life might become for the two of us when our children said good-bye. Ministry rather than money was the important preoccupation for both of us, and we began to ask what form it would take when Gail no longer felt it necessary to remain home every day for the sake of children.

Knowing that Gail has gifts as a teacher of the Scriptures, we created a plan for her accelerated involvement in ministry to people as the children's need for her diminished. She began to increase her reading and study time. As the children grew older and entered high school, she became free to accept increasing numbers of invitations to speak or to visit with people in need of help. She developed her own systems of information storage, her own library, and her own themes of interest. A growing interaction occurred between the two of us as we enjoyed sharing the conclusions of our reading and thinking.

Today as our children prepare to leave us for college, neither of us want to say that good-bye. But already the preliminary stages of their leaving are behind us, and we feel filled with pride by the decisions we've seen them make. We've tried to be there for support when their choices were bad ones and they had to face consequences. And we tried to stay out of the way when they received credit from others, when their choices were good ones. Their leaving should not take a fatal chunk out of their father and mother's lives, because we have new things to do. We have planned them, prayed over them, and we anticipate them with relish. If their leaving is a time of excitement for them, it is a time of anticipation for us also. Sad, to be sure, but nevertheless exciting.

Marjorie Johanson has been a totally committed mother. If her husband, Ken, does not give serious attention to the changes Kirk's leaving makes in her life, he will miss an important opportunity, perhaps the last, to help her fill her life with new challenges. Without him, she will simply drift into middle-life aimlessness (I believe I earlier called it circling the wagons at Denver). Or she will turn to others who will provide her with the stimulus to carve out an independent way of life, possibly in ways that Ken may not fully appreciate. But if they wisely seize the moment, their mid-life marriage may have great years ahead for it.

When Ken and Marjorie Johanson leave at the end of our second visit, they have made plans to spend the evening with Kirk, if he's free. They plan to tell their son that the California trip is not what they would have selected for him, but they'll support his right to include that as one of the possibilities for the fall's plans. Ken will ask for the right to bring up hard questions about the trip, so that Kirk has a chance to foresee all the potential problems ahead. Kirk will also have to face the fact that he'll have to finance California by himself.

That's why no one was more surprised than Kirk Johanson when his parents raised the subject after supper. This time the conversation had a pleasant ending, because Ken and Marjorie delightedly discovered that their son had a deeper grasp of the issues than they had ever surmised. And when Kirk left them to go to his studies, he felt warmed by the realization that his parents would indeed give him the freedom to think through all the options that might face a young man getting ready to say good-bye.

Incidentally, Marjorie Johanson entered art school the same fall her son Kirk started at college. The boy never went to California; the marriage never faltered; and a mid-life home didn't fall apart.

At mid-life we face the challenge to release our children. The Bible records the release of several children by mature and perceptive parents. In each case, the children were quite young. Hannah, for example, faced it when she released her son, Samuel, at a very early age, to the opportunities he would have to grow and become the spiritual leader of a nation. Mordecai released Esther to the palace of a king, and the maturity of their continued relationship allowed him to urge the best from her for many years that followed her point of good-bye. But maybe the mother of our Lord accomplished the most re-markable release of all. Surely, it occurred unusually early in His life, but when her son was twelve, Mary took a routine look around her to locate Jesus in a crowd and found him missing.

Admittedly, Mary at first felt as agitated as any mother, but her feelings quickly became mollified when later He said to her in the temple, "I must be about my father's business. . . ." She immediately understood.

But even Mary gives evidence that release does not come easily to the best of us. She tested her hold over Him at the wedding in Cana of Galilee, when she attempted to direct His actions. She even came one day and stood at the edge of a crowd, hoping to dissuade Him from His mission. The remarks of our Lord indicate that all may not have always been so smooth, and He had to handle her with tenderness, yet firmness. She must say good-bye, and He had to leave to pursue his Father's business.

Two thousand years later, Ken and Marjorie Johanson understand a bit of Mary's uneasiness. It is hard to say good-bye to Kirk, but it is desperately important that they do so, for his sake and for theirs.

10
Life Is Full of Change

If you are Steve and Karen Doyle's neighbor and you look across the yard and see Steve sitting out on his patio, the chances are you'll be impressed with the apparent serenity of the moment. A wisp of smoke and a mouth-watering smell suggest a steak in the barbecue pit; the cut grass and tended flower beds propose order in the homelife; and Steve Doyle's relaxed figure in the garden lounge chair says "tranquility" after a long day's work.

But no tranquility exists in Doyle's mind. The body may say relaxation; but the mind says turmoil, stress, and anger. Why, when all outer circumstances appear to be peaceful, does Steve Doyle seethe inwardly? The answer? seemingly stable relationships suddenly in a state of disintegration.

It is good that Karen Doyle does not ask her husband what is going on in his mind. He would be hard pressed to answer her. He would not fully make sense if he tried to put it into words for her benefit. All he knows is that in the space of a few days three unexpected experiences have entered Stephen Doyle's life: He has been impressed with changes at his college; his young protégé is leaving him for a job in Portland; and his close friend and associate has collapsed with a heart attack.

People and worlds he assumed would always be there have sent a disturbing message: Life is full of change.

Tell Stephen Doyle that life is full of change, and he'll agree with you, intellectually. But like most of us at the noon of life, he's not prepared to deal with the fact emotionally. These were the sort of things that happened to others, and in spite of the fact that one must be rational and objective about changes in life, it still feels bewildering when it happens close to home.

Why the inner disturbance at the college reunion? Why is it bothersome when a college builds new buildings and in the process destroys some old ones?

What bothers Doyle has something to do with the fact that his visible roots are being cut away. College was a kind of "home." Memories of Steve and Karen's first experimentations with adulthood lived there. That place of firsts was being destroyed. Others crowd in on his world of the past. It's *their* world now, as much as it once was his. And as this world grows Steve Doyle seems to shrink in significance and power. Strange as it seems, it bothers Steve Doyle that the university wiped out his old residence in a construction project, not even seeming to care that he had once lived there.

At other times the Doyles had returned to the alma mater and sat and reminisced about events and people symbolized by places. "Remember when we kissed at this corner?" "Do you remember this place, where we had that massive argument?" "Do you recall the time we . . . here?" The symbols that visualize those memories are swiftly passing away. All in the name of progress, expansion, and modernity.

We like change as young adults; we are not so sure what we might like in mid-life. A strange egotism within us suggests that the world should freeze in the wake of our walk through it. It should remain the same in order to maintain our memories, our achievements, our experiences. Then we can go back and recall each place and how it seemed to exist simply for us.

Perhaps at the noon of life we become powerfully aware that we are not so important after all. Each successive generation replaces us, often bettering and expanding upon each of our achievements and experiences. And when they do this, the message that comes to us—whether it be true or false—is that we are just that much more insignificant, dispensable, just a fading part of the landscape.

That disturbs Steve Doyle. Accuse him of it, and he will laugh and deny it. What's going on inside him is not factual or rational; it is emotional. He feels, more than anything else. His relationship with the people and places of the past seem to be dissolving. It makes him feel uneasy, adrift from things that once seemed permanent and dependable. There had always been this feeling that if the present moments turned sour, one could always go back and recall, perhaps experience, some of the old days. But they are gone now; at least the symbols are. And the result is a troubling, gnawing feeling that the past is little more than an illusion—certainly not a place one can flee to when there is need of safety. Steve Doyle doesn't like such feelings.

None of us do. Karen Doyle may not fully appreciate why her husband shows such strong irritation about such "absurdities." Perhaps she doesn't fully appreciate her husband's male perspective at this point. It isn't clear to her that it was back at the campus that Steve may have had his last strong experiences of intimacy with friends. Those are more than memories for Stephen; at college there were other men with whom he had shared the fullness of his young life. They had dreamed together, worked together, discovered new aspects of life together. When one failed, the other knew and shared the bitter moment. When one succeeded, all rejoiced and shouted together.

Stephen has not had friendships and intimacies such as those, apart from his marriage to Karen, since he graduated. Caught up in a life of hard work and achievement, there has not been the time for the sort of camaraderie that marked the college years. There are few times for the mid-life equivalent of a pickup football game, a late night "bull session," a spontaneous venture over to the girls' dorm. The pursuit of business has been a good experience, but something has been lost. It is called intimacy, and while Steve has a hard time defining what that means, he knows it's been lost, and the changes at the college wordlessly remind him of its effect.

For Steve Doyle this inner turbulence is accompanied by a strange kind of loneliness. *Why,* he asks himself sometimes, *do I have no close friends anymore?*

If Karen Doyle does not understand Stephen's reactions, it may be because she has tended to maintain an experience of intimacy. She has experienced it in the raising of two small children, which has created a strong, intimate bond. Because the pursuit of relationship has been her instinct anyway, she has retained touch with certain women and made other friends with whom she shares common experiences. Had she chosen a vocation other than the one of mother, she probably still would have pursued certain relationships. But Steve has not, and the weekend has painfully accented the fact that he is entering the second half of his life with great feelings of aloneness.

Doyle is also troubled about the news he received this morning from a young man in his company who is leaving for Portland. When his mind leaves the college weekend and turns to this turn of events, he once again feels surprised at his attitude. Why isn't he following the objective side of his nature and congratulating his assistant on the seizing of a great opportunity?

Instead of patting his young friend on the back, Steve finds himself trying to raise arguments as to why there will be certain failure in Portland. His mind focuses on the areas where his assistant is inept, unprepared, doomed for failure. Why does he major on these thoughts and not on the optimistic possibilities that Portland affords for his protégé?

Yale's Daniel Levinson would suggest that Doyle is facing the mentor's version of something called the BOOM phenomena (Becoming One's Own Man). Put simply, the assistant who wants to go to Portland has been Steve Doyle's "man." Steve has poured himself into his employee; in Christian terms he has discipled him.

To see his disciple blossom and take on greater amounts of responsibility, to make good decisions, and to extend Doyle's own method and style of doing things has been a source of great satisfaction for Steve Doyle. In part it has substituted for the peer friendships that Steve had enjoyed at college. And it had been a chance to assert direction over another life.

But now the object of all this training and trust chooses to leave. He says that he wants to go to Portland, but Steve hears another message. The assistant speaks about opportunity; Doyle hears rejection. And he does not want to let go.

Stephen Doyle will likely bring to bear a few forms of subtle pressure on his assistant. First he'll try to persuade him that he owes Steve too much to leave him now. And if that doesn't work, Doyle will make subtle cracks that are designed to point out places where the other has not yet mastered the business enough to make it on his own. But if all that fails to crack the determination of his assistant to head for Portland, Stephen may show anger and abruptly separate himself from his disciple. Their parting is not liable to be friendly and mutually affirming.

An unconscious fear may bother Doyle: In Portland, his young assistant may discover that Stephen wasn't the best at what he did, that he can actually be competed with and out-pointed. The young assistant's choosing to leave is a message to Steve that he isn't good enough to keep mastery over his world. Things are slipping away. This signal comes clearer and clearer at the noon of life. Unanticipated and unaccepted, it is a painful message.

If you take another glance at Stephen Doyle in his backyard, you might see a man who has another troublesome thought circling in his mind.

His business partner is a sick man. Chest pains have spoken, and now his associate lies stricken in an Intensive Care Unit. What disturbs Steve as he broods upon this new event? Is it that Steve is going to have to work harder for the coming weeks? Not at all. Is he upset for the welfare of his working friend? Perhaps, but even that is not paramount in Doyle's mind.

His partner's heart attack has brought home a brutal truth that screams for attention more than anything else. The lesson? That all relationships are tentative—and more so from now on in Steve's life. For the first time Stephen Doyle is being confronted with the possibility *and* probability that people will leave him with regularity. His past and the people he remembers abandon him; those into whose life he has made an investment (be they children or protégés) are preparing to leave him, and his friends are capable of leaving him.

His friends? They may leave through company transfers as they become more and more important to their organizations at mid-life. They may choose to leave him because there are better neighborhoods or locations in the world to live. They may leave him by falling behind through failures and accidents. Or like his partner, they may leave him through sickness and death.

For the first time Doyle finds himself reading the obituary page in the newspaper with interest. Occasionally he hears the reports of deaths of people with whom he went to school: heart attacks, suicides, accidents, cancer.

Doyle sits tonight in his backyard and he ponders what is happening. The life-style of his partner is similar to his. They exercise in basically the same way; they have kept essentially the same weight levels; they have worked the same hours. The bottom-line question? Why did it happen to his partner and not to him?

What has happened to his partner in Atlanta is a devastating twofold reminder to Doyle. First his own vulnerability and second that no relationship is either permanent or absolutely dependable.

These are some of the components of mid-life thinking, and they are burdensome to men like Steve Doyle. Is there a root to all of them?

Perhaps it lies in the word *control*. Stephen Doyle is used to living a life that operates most smoothly if it appears to be under his own control. Perhaps control was always a fantasy, but nevertheless gave Doyle much of his confidence up until recent days. His past (strangely enough) was under control of his memory; his business, its assets, and his people seemed under control; his future was under control. But tonight Stephen Doyle has nagging doubts that anything is really under control. And that is why he sits so silently, absorbed in thoughts that have no termination. They go in circles.

Interesting! Steve Doyle may have the same theme of struggle that Ken and Marjorie Johanson are living with down the street. They have to let go of their son, Kirk. Doyle has let go of the past, the protégé, and the partner. He's learning that relationships are valuable, but they are also potentially transient.

It's not that he has to destroy his memories. He just can't live off them. And it's not that he shouldn't grieve over the loss of a protégé. He just cannot hold on to him forever. Finally it's not that he shouldn't feel disturbed over the sudden absence of a stricken partner. He just can't assume the permanence of his peers.

But beyond all that, Steve Doyle has to come to grips with his world. It is slowly reducing him to his real size and significance. And the process brings inner turbulence—not an unusual experience for people living at high noon.

11
Drifters . . . Apart

The night the Johansons confronted their son, Kirk, and Francis King came home from a difficult afternoon with her parents, and Stephen Doyle sat brooding on his patio was the same night Willard and Trish Solomon left their home and went out on the town, as some say. But they did not leave together.

Later during the evening their activities might appear glamorous—in one case [Willard's], daring, and certainly in keeping with the trends of a contemporary world. Willard is with a woman who is not his wife; Trish is with woman friends who are out to take advantage of every cultural event their city offers.

When Willard Solomon joins the young woman from the filing department at the restaurant, he is hard pressed to wonder why he waited so long to make such an encounter happen. What seems to have happened between them in a matter of minutes amazes him. A sudden strange sense of exhilaration rises within him, a seeming renewal of the "mystery of the hunt" that he remembers well from younger days. All his senses are at attention; each moment takes on significance. Why, he asks himself, is this so different from life at home with his wife?

Trish asks herself similar questions as she joins friends for the evening. She is aware of what seems to be a sense of freedom that she has not known for many years. She finds her mind alert and curious about the events of the theater. A few years before this moment she would have admitted to virtually no interest in anything except that which centered on her husband and children. And since Willard had never been interested in experiences such as the theater, she had turned her mind off to such things soon after they married. But now that mind turned on again. Why, she asks herself, is she enjoying an evening so much when Willard, her husband, has nothing to do with it. For the first time in years she is a *Trish* and not merely a *Mrs. Willard Solomon, mother and wife.* The feeling presents alternating senses of guilt and excitement.

The Solomons may be in the visible stages of drifting apart. If so, the drift in relationship had not started that evening; it simply took on a new form of accelerated activity. A deteriorating marriage came out of the closet.

The Solomons illustrate in attitude and performance something of the great mid-life struggle going on in the contemporary marriage relationship. What both are doing this evening simply represents the sorts of things that can happen when people in marriages reach the noon of life and lack the capacity to renew themselves and their relationships.

What's happening in the Solomon home? In the broadest sense, the Solomons are experiencing something that many observers of mid-life see with regularity. Carl Jung was among the first to suggest that male and female share common traits, the male traits of "functioning" and the female traits surrounding relationship and "intimacy."

The male of the species, Jung once proposed, tend to suppress their female, or relational, traits in favor of functioning or achieving, during the first decades of adulthood, in order to establish themselves in terms of self-worth.

Conversely, although the times are admittedly changing, it is likely that young-adult women will give attention to female traits during the same period of life, centering on the pursuit of stable relationships and the intimacy they appear to promise. To what extent these male and female pursuits are culturally implanted is a constant debate.

Willard Solomon, for example, was most likely quite pleased with the balance of his life for the first fifteen years he was married to Trish. She kept their home in order, maintained the children in proper behavior, and provided the nurturing warmth and affection he needed when he came to her. But Willard's center of preoccupation in life was in his career, where he was consumed with the ambitions of professional advancement and financial leverage.

But now things have changed; the career, once meteoric, is leveling off, and Willard Solomon finds himself feeling a bit empty in spirit. Probe his thoughts, and you will discover that he feels cheated, but he doesn't know who did the cheating.

In lonely moments he sits brooding like a teenager, staring into space. He watches a beer commercial on television: happy, vibrant, attractive people his age. And he knows he would not fit into their company, in spite of the fact that he envies, even craves, what they call "gusto." Why, Willard asks himself, does he have no close friends? Why does life with Trish seem so routine, in fact, boring? Why does it seem that no one really responds to him, apart from his managerial role in the company and as a parent or a husband in the home? Who really listens to and really knows the "real him"?

Trish, on the other hand, was only too willing to participate in this arrangement that her husband now finds boring. The maintenance of the home and the raising of her children was something she'd been taught was right and proper, and she felt happy in the pursuit. She had been content to be the arranger of the home schedule, the family "nurse" or "cheerleader" in moments of pain and triumph, the communicator who stood in the middle of conflicts and possibilities, and the happy, ever-ready lover when affection of any kind was needed. Her life had been that of a "reactor" to the initiatives of her children and her husband. It had been a good and respectable style of life, but suddenly its benefits appeared to have fallen short. With her husband increasingly busy and her children leaving home, Trish had little left but to keep redecorating her house and rearranging the furniture and the centerpieces. Nice, but not enough.

The time has come to want to *do* something of her own volition—something that centered around her own needs and curiosities, something that belonged solely to her. She wanted to master something that might bring a new awareness of personal dignity and identity to her life. Like Willard, who is searching for a new intimacy, Trish is discovering the search for the masculine side of her life. For all practical purposes, that side had remained dormant within her for more than twenty years. And that needn't have happened. It is the product of a deficient marriage, the consequences of which are going to show in the noon of life.

What is happening now at high noon can only be called a dramatic crossover of the traits. Willard is beginning to be unconsciously aware of his need for greater amounts of intimacy, just as Trish is beginning to ask if there aren't new experiences of learning and achievement that go beyond her home. And neither is prepared to meet the other's need. Why? Because they were not prepared for what was to happen and because they had drifted too far out of touch to understand the dynamics of it all.

This is why Willard and Trish have entered separate pathways. He needs someone to respond to him; she seeks something worthwhile to do. Why can't Willard and Trish talk this out? Why can't he tell her what he is thinking and feeling? And why can't Trish explain her frustration to Willard? Why is she reluctant to express her sense of emptiness to him?

Perhaps it is because they have frozen their images of each other. Willard will always see Trish as a mother and wife, whose primary interests are in home building. And Trish cannot pick up the signals of Willard's loneliness and self-doubt beneath his life-style as a hard-working, ever-confident sales manager. They no longer understand each other's personal language. *It becomes easier for each of them to reach out to new people, whose perceptions of them are not overgrown with the images of the past.*

Relational boredom and stagnancy are the poisons of a mid-life marriage. One sees it regularly. A woman comes to visit me at my study. Actually she would like to gain my approval or at least my sympathy, as her pastor, for her intention to separate from her husband.

"Why," I ask, "are you ready to terminate a marriage that is twenty-four years in length?"

She relates the description of a home where life has drifted into a suffocating routine. "My husband is content to come home at the end of every day and sit. Just simply sit! Watch television and go to bed. There is little to talk about. He has little desire to try anything novel: new foods, new experiences, new friends. He has even lost his interest in sex."

She goes on to talk about the excitement she experiences in new relationships and opportunities at her work. What finally comes through in the conversation, however, is the admission that she has been seeing a man in another department of her company, and he has excited her curiosity. Lunches together have extended to occasional evening dates; random touches have moved toward more intense intimacy. She is, she admits, feeling what she calls "young" again.

It will be very hard for her to go back again to the old commitments after this. There is no feeling of vitality at home, she says, only responsibility. And the world in which she lives has relatively little respect for such commitment and responsibility, when pleasure and novelty are at stake.

What has happened in these failing relationships? Let me suggest several possibilities.

First, and most obviously, the Solomons share a marriage that has simply stopped growing. In fact it stopped a long time ago. As marriage partners they have become cut flowers. The bloom may still be evident, but no life remains in the stem.

In earlier years Willard Solomon had never stopped to ask himself what Trish might be interested in doing with her life as her responsibilities as a mother began to reach a termination point, with the children leaving for college. Trish, enclosed in her world at home, had lost touch with Willard's inner life and had mistaken busy-ness with inner health. She never perceived that he could be a lonely man.

My wife, Gail, and I have a memory of an afternoon when our children came in from school, threw their books on the table, and prepared to rush back out the door, for play with their friends. It was a poignant moment as Gail recognized that the children had nothing to tell her and didn't need to be with her. Sadly she turned to me and said, "The kids don't need me anymore." A slightly exaggerated statement, but nevertheless an accurate assessment of a mother's feelings. Gail was headed toward forced retirement.

As a husband and wife, we began to see the need to plan her second "career." And lay plans we did, so that with increasing amounts of time she could become a speaker and teacher, an author, and a counselor. The result? She never stopped growing, and new avenues of life began to open up. But we had planned for the noon hours of life when it was still mid-morning.

A second destructive element in mid-life marriages can be the feeling of the loss of what some call romance. Here we are reflecting upon the emotional strands of a relationship. They are short strands, to be sure, and easily forgotten as marriages gather years. But without the injection of emotional renewal, a dullness of response between people becomes a habit. Physical touch brings little excitement; the eyes convey no mysterious messages; laughter disappears.

Why does this happen? Perhaps a false feeling of the security of a commitment makes some men and women take each other for granted. There is a loss of motivation to attract or to "win" the other. Each loses interest in reaching out to please a partner through physical attractiveness, sexual affection, and the sort of admiration that causes one to grow in self-worth.

When this loss takes place, it is simply too easy for partners to begin to withdraw first to their fantasy world and create mental scenarios of romance and pleasure with others. In many cases this leads to a willingness to translate fantasy to reality. And in a world in which the slogan seems to be that "everyone is doing it," it is not at all difficult for a bored man or woman to experiment with alternative relationships in which the "electricity" will return.

Willard Solomon is living out his fantasy in the restaurant tonight. And the response to his attentiveness by the woman with whom he shares the evening makes it easy for him to wonder what took him so long to follow the advice of others who said it was such a pleasurable alternative to what he was living with. This seems like romance to Willard, in a way he'd not experienced it for years.

For Trish the romance may not be sexual in orientation. But it is the romance of events, of being where there is movement and excitement. Just being there brings her to a feeling of self-worth she has not felt for years. It cracks the door of her curiosity to ask what other things are in store for her. Others are providing the impetus for her to seek emotional renewal in a way Willard never thought to do.

If the Solomon marriage is in a state of drift, it may be, thirdly, because Trish and Willard forgot how to talk to each other. To be sure, they exchanged many words. But the vocabulary was that of facts, reports, and events. The subject matter was of bills, of things, of children, of obligations.

But inner feelings, dreams, struggles, disappointments, and spiritual questions were missing—perhaps because life had become too busy to cultivate the atmosphere in which such subjects can be discussed; perhaps because Willard hadn't taken the time to ask the right questions; or perhaps because Trish had not taken the time to stop her routines, when Willard came home, in order to listen.

But now that there is enough money to pay bills, now that the children are leaving home, and now that there is time to get things done, what do Willard and Trish have to negotiate? They can go their own way. Nothing to talk about. What talk is necessary can be done with others.

The Solomons may weather the storm of this evening. Many have. After a few evenings with the company file clerk, Willard may realize that the relationship has limits that he cannot pass. And Trish may discover that the beneficial growth she seeks cannot be pursued at the expense of her marriage. It is possible, but the longer they wait to investigate the possibilities, it becomes less and less probable.

At mid-life most marriages face a certain shock. The changes in surrounding circumstances will bring to the surface hidden values, potentials, and flaws. Only a married couple expecting such surprises will be ready to take them on as they come and ride the changes to higher levels of understanding and intimacy.

Willard needs a wife who will join him in his quest for newer intimacy. Trish needs a husband who will encourage her exploration into new worlds of discovery and achievement. And unless both are willing to make such a reach toward the other, there will be trouble.

But if they make the reach, the marriage at the noon of life offers enormous potential for satisfaction. There is increasing liberty of time and space, freedom from the need to prove oneself, and the stability of a basic relationship that has weathered the storms of the years and has proven dependable and durable. Perhaps it has inadequacies, but those are known and can be worked with.

Willard and Trish Solomon have a great future ahead of them, but they are going to have to go back home and discover it together. And that's where they should be that night.

12
My Mother, My Father

Frances King is forty-one years old, and she tells her friends that while the birth certificate claims it, her feelings deny it. "I know my body says 'forty,' but my mind says 'college girl.'"

There would be very little, apart from the certificate, that would betray Frances, if she wanted to claim a younger age. She looks younger, owns a vivacious personality that exudes a spirit of youthfulness, and her tastes in life-style point toward an affinity with a more carefree generation. Frances King does not seem to be a candidate for mid-life thoughts, let alone what some call crises.

But in her life one dramatic exception exists. It has to do with her parents. Born when her parents were in their late thirties, Frances King was known as a mid-life baby. The result: Frances at forty-one has parents who are nearing eighty, and aging has been harsh upon them.

In the extreme sense, she typifies what can happen to some at the noon of life: She has become her parents' "parent." It is more than an uncomfortable experience.

Several things have faced Frances and her husband, Charles, all at once. First, she uneasily watches two people on whom she'd once depended for parental leadership lose a vital hold on their own lives. The growing awareness that Frances might have to allocate increasing amounts of time to attending to her parents and their needs follows. That time will have to be taken away from her own children and family interests, at the expense of events and experiences she had selfishly looked forward to as her children reached the upper school years. Again, it is a quantity of time she wishes she could have free to be with her husband, Charles.

Other issues bring upset to Frances after her visit to her parents' home. There is the anguish of making painful decisions she knows her aged parents will not like, because they are no longer able to make the well-considered judgments, regarding their financial and home situation, that once would have been clear to them.

But perhaps the underlying struggle facing Frances King is the realization that her personal intimacy with her parents is slowly disintegrating. Unresolved issues that existed between her and her mother and father over the years now are enlarging, and they are frequently raised in tense moments. What was often brushed over, diplomatically covered up in the past, is not so easily handled now, because Frances's mother is in a stage of aging where her words match her exact thoughts. What Frances often hears when she is with her mother are words of anger, hurt, or accusation. Frances's mother appears to have a selective memory and can often raise incidents from the past that her daughter would like to forget and wishes she'd taken pains to resolve before now.

The result is that Frances King lives with the guilt of an obligatory relationship to her parents. There is love for them, but she has to fight the temptation to feel her actions in caring for them spring less out of honor and affection than purely family responsibility.

Not all people in mid-life will face the full force of Frances King's situation. But most of us will wrestle with hard questions concerning the relationship we have with the older generation. Until now our parents have stood between us and the grave; they have been the mark of stability and consistency upon which most of us could depend. We always had the quiet suspicion that if life caved in upon us, we could run back to them for some sort of refresher course, an overhaul, certainly a hand of assistance. But what may happen to more than a few in the noon of life (as it happened in extreme to Frances King) is that we suddenly discover, through no one's fault, that our parents begin to look to us for the sort of support we expected of them.

In the best of families this can be a remarkably fruitful period of life for parent and offspring—a time of loving candor and sharing. Parent and son or daughter become friends in the richest sense of that word's meaning. The mid-lifer has come into the fuller realization of the challenges his parents faced, and there is no longer the need for either generation to prove anything to the other. Identity and independence have been established; separation has occurred; some kind of achievement has been recognized. In some cases real friendship may only now begin.

It is not unusual for the man or woman entering the noon of life to feel a sudden urge to reach backward into the meaning of the parental relationship. In one's twenties and thirties so much energy is exerted to establish who one is and what one can do, that there is a tendency to almost repudiate one's childhood and the parents who controlled it in the force of the forward look. But identity and achievement having been established, many mid-lifers begin a wistful looking back.

One experiences new interest in family roots, the themes of one's bringing up, questions about why parents did what they did in the family process. Now one is not ashamed of the past; in fact there may be intense curiosity.

When I was in my fortieth year, I was invited to speak at a retreat for men. During the first evening supper, I overheard an extremely aged man at the other end of the table ask someone who I was. Upon learning that I was the speaker, he came over, sat down beside me, and introduced himself as a retired minister who had been pastor to my mother's family more than sixty years ago.

He began to recall stories of my mother's childhood as part

of a Swedish immigrant family—powerful stories of hardship and suffering, pleasure and joy. I was transfixed, and my curiosity caused him to talk in response to my questions for almost two hours.

Why, I later asked myself, had I never sought out those stories before? If I'd have been interested, my mother would have told them all to me at a much earlier time. The simple truth: I wasn't interested! Only the present and the future had seized my attention. And only at mid-life, when I began to see life in a more balanced fashion, could I experience the freedom of going back to my roots and finding out what was there.

When I returned home from that retreat, I phoned my mother to tell her about my remarkable experience with her childhood pastor and how moved I had been to hear so much of her early years. Not long after, I received a cassette tape recording from her, filling in even more of the blanks of a family history I'd never known or appreciated until now.

On another day I met a woman who had served my family as an almost permanent babysitter when I was an infant. As she began to unfold tales of my childhood, I found myself giving rapt attention to experiences that would either have embarrassed or bored me at an earlier state in my adulthood. When we parted, I asked her if she would be willing to take the time to write me a long letter recounting her memories of those days. Some months later, the letter came, and it is among my personal treasures today. Only at the noon of life did the desire to go back and recover the roots of parental and family relationships exist.

But this desire to recover the past may not always be a happy experience. For in the look backward may come the uncovering of relational realities between parent and child that may not be pleasant to rediscover.

Not infrequently we have blocked off unpleasant memories of family experiences that were once so destructive or painful that the mind buried them. At mid-life, old issues long unresolved often surface. We remember harsh words, tragic conflicts, moral inconsistencies, the absence of affection or

affirmation. And with the raising of the memories can come renewed feelings of anger and resentment.

Thus in the very period of time when parents and offspring
should become friends of a deeper sort, greater cleavage may
occur because one or both generations do not want to face the
pain of the past.

Perhaps at mid-life there is a greater need to engage in the
loving act of forgiveness between the generations than there
has been at any other time. Now each generation can see the
other in real terms. A father or mother is no longer an unreal
hero, but the real human being that all parents actually are.
And a son or daughter is no longer the unappreciative rebel,
but one who has tried hard, in most cases, to perpetuate the
family ideal in the best way he or she knows how.

In many cases our modern culture has not made the relationship between mid-lifers and their parents an easy matter. The
tendency of people in the Western world to establish a dramatic independence between the generations comes at the expense of the so-called extended family that the Bible knew so
well. Today parents and children often live thousands of miles
from each other. A person's career, rather than family loyalty,
will usually determine place of residence.

Because we live a high-paced life-style in the Western world,
relationships in the family are often considered a second- or
third-priority matter. Parents and children become drastically
different from each other in values, living standards, spiritual
and intellectual interest, and emotional structure. Thus, parent-child relationships at mid-life can move between the
extremes of virtual uninterest to intense involvement. And
the involvement or the lack of interest can come from either
generation.

Perhaps the first great theme of mid-life, in terms of parental
relationships, should be that of reaching out to touch one's parents. Is there the chance to make friends? If unresolved tensions have been addressed, the answer can often be a beautiful
yes.

Frances King faces the question of mid-life parental relationships at its extreme. When we sit together, I suggest that she has to think with certain themes in mind.

First, she must remember that her primary priority is her husband and her children. Her parents had long ago released her to that relationship. They could not seize her back. Then she must think and act toward her parents as she knows they would have wanted her to when they saw their world in a larger perspective.

"Frances," I ask her, "what would your father and mother have wanted you to do about their financial situation and their physical problems if you'd asked them these questions ten years ago?"

"I know very well what they would have wanted me to do then. They would want me to do exactly what I'm doing now," she answers.

"Then be careful to do exactly what you know they would have wanted you to do. And even if in their present state of mind they complain beyond reason, remind yourself that you love them enough to do what's best for them, just as they once did what was best for you."

Perhaps Frances King will take my advice and assurance. But it will not alleviate the pressure she is going to feel. And for a few years she is going to have to carefully budget her time and priorities, perhaps even at the expense of some of her personal desires.

If we resent these responsibilities, it may be that we must blame our culture for suggesting that our personal freedom was so great that it could be pursued at the expense of our loved ones.

Frances faces a challenge—not an easy one—that all mid-lifers must encounter: the question of whether we are servants or kings. For some mid-lifers the call to servanthood may be a part of life that brings great reward. If not now, then.

Section V

Reflections on Mid-Life Spirituality

13
The Tightrope Moments

Some years ago a troupe of tightrope walkers known as the Flying Wallendas performed at the circus in Detroit's Cobo Hall. The Wallendas were famous for their creation of an incredible human pyramid—three levels of people making their way across the wire from one side of the arena to the other.

The crowd would sit each night in awed silence as four men walked the wire, three more men standing on poles mounted on the walkers' shoulders. And above those three, a woman sat on a chair. Those who saw the human pyramid act never forgot the drama of the moment.

One night, things on the wire went wrong, and tragedy suddenly struck the Wallendas. As I recall the story, it happened somewhere just beyond the midpoint of the wire, when the knees of one of the walkers, Dieter Wallenda, began to quiver. The balancing pole he carried started to seesaw. Then the crowd heard his anguished cry, *"Ich kahn nicht mehr halten"* (I can't hold on any longer).

Dieter Wallenda's loss of control toppled the entire pyramid. An instant later the formation collapsed, most of the performers hurtling to the floor, some suffering permanent injury. Others managed to grab on to the wire until help could arrive. The horrifying spectacle revealed what happens on the high wire when one person is unable to maintain his share of the load. Everyone in the act was affected.

I have recounted the story of the Wallendas on many occasions because I have thought it to be a parable about the mystery of human experience and relationship. We are all performers on "high wires" of sorts, and as the years of our lives accumulate the seriousness of the implications of our walk increases. Slips in earlier years mean relatively little; but accidents at middle life can have dramatic consequences. For not only are we liable to suffer injurious consequences, but it is likely that, should we falter, others who are part of our "pyramid" will also suffer with us. That's why I think the story of the high-wire walker is the mid-lifer's story, an especially apt parable when one ponders the spiritual dimensions of the afternoon of life.

When I think of the man on that wire, I see a metaphor of pressure, and it is pressure a man or a woman in the middle of life can appreciate. On the wire, for example, one must toe the line, with very little tolerance for error. Of course it wasn't always necessary to be that exact. When the performer was an infant, just the act of walking was an effort. Then his parents affirmed him for the mere taking of a baby step. But now walking means careful, agile steps on an almost invisible line. There must be perfect balance, no wavering. And, of course, he cannot return to the place from whence he first came. Once the walker is out on the wire, he is committed—no turning back. The picture grows more vivid when I think that on the high wire, the walker carries a great weight (those above him), and he is locked into an arrangement with the others who walk in front and behind. He must not only do his part perfectly, but he must do it in tandem with the others who share the load.

Add to all this the final fact that he does it again and again in front of great crowds who will watch him succeed or fail. In part it is their applause he seeks. But on that night in Detroit, Dieter Wallenda played to their horror.

That sad picture of the tightwire walker who could no longer hold on gives me the starting point for what I think is the most important of the dimensions of middle life—spiritual reality. There is no point in brooding on the afternoon of life unless, sooner or later, we ask about its spiritual implications. In fact everything discussed in this book so far finds its origin in the spiritual perspective.

More than anything else, I believe the middle life experience to be a spiritual one. Mid-life drives us to wrestle with spiritual questions one way or another. If we are willing to face them, the chances are that we will become deeper persons, conscious of a "world" within us that we have most likely left unexplored for most of our lives. But if we are unwilling to confront these questions, then mid-life can become a flight away from the inner world to things outside us, which promise for a moment to be our salvation.

The longer we live, the higher the "wire" we walk seems to become. The longer we live, the heavier our sense of responsibility for the people in our pyramid. The longer we live, the greater the sense of pressure to make it from one end to the other. And all this makes one cast about for resources and capacities—strength, wisdom, courage, balance, pace, direction. Where will such things come from? The answer? They should come primarily from the inner spirit of the human being. But the temptation will come to seek these resources and capacities from outside ourselves, not from within. That is an important matter for us to decide.

Many at mid-life do not understand the reality of the inner spirit, especially those of us who have spent so much of the morning of our lives building up the resources that exist on the surface. This inner spiritual reality can seem strange to many of us. It is almost as if someone needed to identify, to define for us, that often indescribable element called the spirit.

So what is this illusive part of us called the inner spirit, which demands attention from many on the high wire at middle life? I call it the spirit, while others are more comfortable by identifying it with the word *soul.* The spirit or the soul cannot be located as if it were an organ of the body, and it is almost impossible to define it in a precise way so that one knows where its boundary lines begin or end. It is just there. The Bible says that God "breathed" it into the first man and woman. It made them separate from the animals.

The inner spirit of a person virtually defies definition because it is so utterly vast, perhaps infinite. We seem to be talking about a dimension of reality that transcends depth, height, and width. Perhaps it is simply best regarded as inner space.

We have learned a lot about outer space in the past few decades, and we know that outer space is infinite, expanding (so it seems) all the time. But it may just be possible that inner space (this spiritual part of us) is just as infinitely expandable.

If outer space remains basically unexplored, it could be said that the inner space of human beings is also inadequately charted. Perhaps the old Christian mystics did as much as anyone to open up inner space, but today their insights are sadly ignored by all but a few. We have traded their information for the data turned up on the mind, the body, the material world about us, and all the time we have ignored the depths within ourselves in which lie the most important insights as to why we are the way we are and, more importantly, what we are capable of becoming at any age.

At best our understanding of our inner worlds, this spirit of ours, is something like the perceptions of the ancient mapmakers who, when unknowledgeable about unexplored areas of the world, would simply draw dragons and monsters upon their maps to note the untraveled ocean and land masses. Those grotesque figures symbolized the fear and the mystery of the unknown. That is the way many of us feel when we monitor the strange signals rising up within, from an inner place we know is there but that is never quite opened up or understood.

Jesus Christ understood the good news and the bad news of inner space, and He was referring to it when He noted the propensity for evil that can come from within. "From within a person . . . evil comes," he said (*see* Mark 7:21, 23). In spite of the fact that He loved people without condition, He was very much aware of the potential of the inner spirit and its capacity for evil or good. Thus it was in the area of the spirit that He concentrated His attention. Conversely, those who were more interested in the surface of the human experience, such as the issues of wealth and power, gave Him little of their time or attention. Little attention, that is, until He threatened what was important to them.

I feel it is worth taking the time and space to identify this important spiritual dimension of personhood because I feel convinced that at mid-life many people come suddenly to a sense of alertness about it, even though they may not understand their thinking in such terms.

Most likely the mid-lifer is thinking spiritually when he or she comes to a moment like that of the high-wire walker who cannot hold on any longer. Halfway across the wire (what we've called the afternoon of life) we become increasingly aware that the slightest slip in various sectors of our life can have catastrophic implications. We cannot afford to waver; yet we face moments that threateningly suggest the inevitability of a slip. We may experience frequent feelings of fear, panic, and the sinking sense that equilibrium is almost gone.

People in the afternoon of life certainly are not suffering from an epidemic of personal misery, but the fact is that more people cry out *"Ich kahn nicht mehr halten"* in the afternoon of life than any of us realize. Usually the words are said silently and are understood only by those who take the time and effort to hear them. Indeed many slip on the wire, and every once in a while there are the sad spills to the ground. Self-esteem becomes diminished; marriages crack open. The will to reach personal potential is destroyed; dreams self-destruct.

Under the pressure of the mid-life walk on the wire, not a few people begin to launch a series of quiet questions that have been avoided or ignored for many, many years. The questions center on the meaning of the "walk," the resources to finish it, and the strength to maintain balance on the way. And from what source do the answers come? From within or without? These are the primary spiritual questions.

Why is spiritual thinking often ignored until mid-life? Perhaps it has something to do with the raw optimism with which we live in the morning hours of life. In the earlier periods, there exists a seeming assurance that all challenges and potentials can be handled in one way or another. We move on enthusiasm, the encouragement of our mentors, the seemingly unlimited "second chances," and the remarkable reservoirs of strength that permit something almost like a trial-and-error style of life.

It is by no means unusual to meet those who—refining these techniques—will walk the wire of life year after year and never show signs of slipping. In a sense one does not know whether to envy or pity such people, because few of us are ever prompted to explore the inner space of our lives until moments of slippage threaten our successful passage on the wire.

If we have begun to think spiritually before mid-life, it is usually because some major event has confronted us with the mystery of human existence or some experience of personal helplessness: personal tragedy, for example, death, defeat, great decisions with enormous consequences, the birth of a child, emotional stress, a long-term illness that saps human endurance. These force a man or a woman to begin looking for levels of reality otherwise ignored when events in life are moving predictably and under personal control.

The Old Testament offers a poignant example of two men who faced high-wire moments in their lives. The ultimate consequences both finally lived with shed enormous light on the earlier choices they made as examples of spiritual thinking. Their names? Abraham and his nephew, Lot.

Having left their homes and journeyed westward from Ur of the Chaldees, both men enjoyed a substantial amount of success and its resulting wealth. But there came a point where a division of their business interests became necessary. Abraham saw the issues clearly and proposed to Lot that they divide assets and move in different directions. Lot, Abraham proposed, could make the initial decision regarding direction. What way would he like to go? Abraham, then, would settle for whatever land Lot did not select.

How Lot made his choice is instructive. It reveals something of the nature of his spiritual (or nonspiritual) thinking. Seeking to expand his fortune and secure it, he looked southward and chose the fertile plains of Sodom. It was an obvious decision for a person whose primary instincts pointed toward the external spaces of life. The good life, he assumed, was to be found by being in the right place, knowing the best people, trading with the proper currencies, seizing the most promising opportunities. On the other hand, what living on the plains of Sodom might do to his soul (and the souls of those in his family) never seems to have occurred to Lot when he made his choice.

One is reminded of some of the final words of Robert Frost's poem:

> Two roads diverged in a wood, and I—
> I took the one less traveled by,
> And that has made all the difference.

Ironically, Lot in this case may have taken the road *most* frequently traveled by those not inclined to spiritual thinking. And those who know what happened later at Sodom realize that Lot's choice did indeed make all the difference.

But Abraham was a different sort of man. You could say that his primary concern was inner space—knowing and obeying his God. The sort of thinking that I am calling spiritual thinking led him to settle for less attractive lands. They weren't the fertile plains that Lot chose, but the lands were adequate for altar building, the basis of Abraham's relationship to God and of His purposes for his life.

Lot traveled southward to Sodom, and before long he found himself not merely living on the plains near Sodom but right in the city itself. What began as a seemingly innocent business decision marked his entire life and the lives of those in his family. When the city of Sodom ultimately experienced the judgment fires of God, Lot lost everything in the debacle—including, for all practical purposes, his family. He typifies the central point I am trying to make about spiritual reality in mid-life. He or she who moves into the afternoon of life placing primary values on external things will grow increasingly devoid of orderly and fruitful inner space.

Abraham, on the other hand, avoided the Sodoms of his generation and moved through what seemed to be an arid country, regularly building altars to God and all the time increasing his holdings through heaven's blessings. A New Testament writer looking back on Abraham's life, said of him and other saints that they desired ". . . a better country, that is, a heavenly one. Therefore God is not ashamed to be called their God, for he has prepared for them a city" (Hebrews 11:16 RSV).

Abraham not only outdistanced Lot in every conceivable business situation, but he deepened and matured in his spirit until he became the father of a great spiritual nation—the nation of Israel. The two men are powerful examples of the sorts of choices we make during the mid-life passage and the resulting consequences experienced on the high wire. Lot ultimately slipped and fell; Abraham walked on with agility and grace. A small slip here and there, but no devastating collapse. The crowd has always been horrified over Lot's sad end; it applauds Abraham's remarkable performance.

These two men provide a wide contrast for us to remember as we ponder the spiritual dimensions of the afternoon of life. It is clear to me that their key decision, upon parting from one another, is not unlike the cluster of decisions many of us make as we approach mid-life. Whether or not we realize it, we are very much like these two men. Where will the base of life's operations be established for the remainder of our years? Will it be the plains of Sodom, where externally speaking, everything looks promising and safe? Or will it be the Abrahamic adventure that trusts in the inner guidance of God, an adventure that may appear to some to be occasionally shaky and risky but that nevertheless pays off because God keeps promises to those who see things His way.

The choices as the wire gets higher and higher? There seem to be several. Let me illustrate some of them in the high-wire experience of a New Testament personality who also had hard choices to make.

Like Abraham, and unlike Lot, Saint Paul was a spiritual thinker, and it showed in his tightwire moments. One of the most dramatic occurred when he landed in the Roman jail for what were possibly the final days of his life. In a letter to the Philippian Christians, he reveals his attitudes toward several significant questions that seem to surface regularly in mid-life spiritual thinking.

The first had to do with his circumstances. He was trapped! Trapped in a jail that probably was hardly larger than a few square yards. And this was the sudden limitation of a man who'd become used to traveling the world, moving among people in new places, coming and going as he pleased, doing and choosing not to do as he felt best. *Now he was trapped!*

One usually first becomes acquainted with the feeling of "trappedness" in the afternoon of life—trapped in a vocation from which there seems to be no release; trapped, perhaps, in a relationship; trapped in a style of personality or temperament that appears unchangeable.

This brings a feeling of psychic suffocation, and with it comes a whirlwind of temptation to want to escape. Many mid-lifers will first succumb to that temptation in the world of fantasy. The daydreaming of adolescence returns, and great images of lost opportunities, "what might have beens" begin to crowd the screen of the mind.

Mid-lifers experience the awareness of closing doors within a vocational field and the occasional questions of what might have happened if one had sought another alternative when there were decisions about vocation still to be made. This seems especially intensified if one's friends appear to have made right decisions and seem to be sailing right through mid-life with every symbol of success and happiness gathering to them.

Trapped with our choices. *Why didn't I go to a better school when I had the chance? Study harder when I went? Date more men (or women) when I had the chance? Develop relationships that I have no more time to develop? Travel more?* Trappedness can create a pile of seeming regrets.

We may feel closed in if we are involved in a marital relationship that shows sagging vitality. We are seeing an increasing number of women, for example, who—having finished the role of mother—are turning their minds toward new endeavors: jobs, the arts, creative activities. Sometimes the effort is based upon the frantic need to flee a perceived trap.

One woman sits in my study and says to me, "My husband has become a boring person. He doesn't want to go anywhere, learn anything new, make new friends. How can I live within a marriage where there is so much to do and see and know that my husband has no interest in any of it? Do you think I have to close down my options simply because he won't come along?"

I ask questions. Was her husband boring when they first married? No, of course not, she says. He was full of potential as a person, and he was loaded with enthusiasm and ambition for a future in the family and in his vocation. When I ask what she thinks has happened, she acknowledges that at least two things have occurred. First, in her opinion, he has stopped growing, wanting to take risks, discover new things. And she doesn't know why. But second, she herself has awakened to all sorts of potentials she never knew about before. She would like to get on with life and can't. She feels trapped married to him.

She provokes searching and difficult questions for which there are few adequate or simple answers. Perhaps the problem can be resolved through joint conversations between the three of us. But there is no doubt that we are starting out with one person (maybe both) feeling terribly limited in a relationship that was originally designed to maximize their freedom for growth and development as persons.

The temptation for her is, of course, to escape—to run as fast as she can from the relationship. On this occasion I quietly ask, "And where or to whom might you run?" When prodded, she finally admits that she has come into contact with someone who offers promising experiences of the kind she wants. And that, she admits, intensifies her struggle.

Her feeling of trappedness in the marriage grows because she thinks there is a way of life beyond that marriage that would bring her what she needs or wants. *Think,* I observe to her, is a key word, and we talk more about the energy of fantasy when one feels locked in this way.

Probably more than once Saint Paul pondered about getting out of his jail in Rome and what he might do if he were free to move again.

Sometimes the mid-lifer feels trapped in a style of personality and temperament. "I just don't seem to be able to change the prevailing attitudes with which I grew up," one says. "Is there no chance of change?"

Many of us have lived through the morning of life nursing along the fantasy that somewhere along the line we would be able to escape what we knew to be character flaws, personality tendencies that are an embarrassment to us. "When I grow up, I'll . . . ," we say to ourselves. But then suddenly we realize *we have grown up.* It would appear that there is no more room for change. We are trapped with what we are.

Like the tightwire walker who is limited by the arrangement of poles and bars and cannot move in any direction but forward to the end of his choices, the mid-lifer takes tentative steps in the only direction that his choices will permit. So every day he rises to go toward a job he may or may not like, makes plans for the weekend with a spouse he may or may not enjoy being with, and lives with internal reactions and personal habit patterns he may secretly wish he could repudiate and modify. And there remains this occasional overwhelming feeling that the rest of life is going to be nothing more than a repetition of today. Options and alternatives have been closed down; control of life has been forfeited.

The trapped feeling is a cousin of another mid-life question—one centering on personal significance. On the high wire, it will cause anyone to lose balance for a moment when the thought surges through the mind and heart. I keep on wondering if Paul in his jail cell did not occasionally ask himself whether it was possible to do anything of significance in his incarcerated condition. We ought not to assume that the answer came as easily as some are quick to think it did. What do I mean by *significance?*

Years ago a doctor friend of mine counseled that I should never enter the church pulpit to preach until I had asked this question of the sermon I'd prepared: "What difference does it make?" Our Western culture has communicated to us the feeling that each of us should make some sort of difference to our generation and to those beyond us. So we ask ourselves: *What difference do I make as a person, and what difference does what I'm doing make in this world of mine?*

As infants we unconsciously assumed that we alone were the only person in the world worth worrying about, and when it appeared to us that others didn't know that, we shrieked and screamed until others got our message. Perhaps in the afternoon of life that false assumption is so dashed to pieces that some are tempted to come to the opposite conclusion nursed along in infancy: We now make no difference whatsoever as people or in accomplishments. Both extreme assumptions are of course patently false. But they are nevertheless real to the one who assumes them.

So a battle goes on in the inner space of many men and women in the afternoon of life. And it has to do with this question of destiny or difference. Will we settle for ordinariness or averageness (as many others seem to be doing), or will we continue the challenge to make sure that something we have done or are doing makes its mark upon our world?

Is there temptation on the part of some of us, during the morning hours of life, to think that history will change because of our existence? That we shall provide the last word on some great question? Change the course of some particular movement? Outdistance the participants in some category of career or discipline? And in the passage of time do some of us come to the realization that there are few (if any) new ideas, that there is always someone better or willing to work harder or longer at things than we are, that organizations can really get along without us?

A friend of mine had a serious heart attack a few years ago, and I did not see him for almost a year while he pursued seclusion and healing. When I saw him again, I asked him what he thought was the most important lesson he'd learned from his experience. His response was instructive: "I learned that when a person falls, the rest of the world goes marching on by, and as it passes, it doesn't miss a footstep."

There are moments in the afternoon of life when the message is whispered into our ear that we are *not* significant and that we are indeed replaceable ants on the human anthill. The message comes when a friend falls in death, someone we admired is suddenly fired, or when we see others, of the younger generation, poised to take our place.

This sort of depressing theme gives way to quiet questions such as "What has all this meant?" And the question of meaning is a sharp departure from the questions of an earlier stage in life. The mid-lifer has been used to struggling with questions such as "How can I succeed?" "Who can I get to know?" "How much can I acquire?" "How important can I become?" or "Who knows and recognizes what I have done?" Now, in the afternoon of life, meaning and enduring value become important. Again, will this person I am and the things I am doing make a difference?

As Saint Paul looked out from prison bars or (to maintain my metaphor) struggled on his high wire he may have been tempted to ask this question because he seemed so limited to maintain his established rhythm of planting the Christian church. Others were free to move toward places with people to whom he would have dearly loved to have ministered. And those others' motives might be questionable. He must have entertained the temptation to feel passed by.

I remember a similar moment not long ago when in attendance at a large conference of leaders, I learned that many of my friends had been quietly invited to gather for a special, unannounced function. Those who had called the meeting and put together the list of invitees had not thought to include me. I remember well the momentary bitter taste of not being asked, the symbolic statement being, You're not important enough to count. Perhaps there was truth to their conclusion; then again maybe someone just forgot about me.

Every one of us have had such moments. And they hurt if we are out on that wire: the mother whose teenagers leave her out of a discussion, an activity she would like to have joined; the mid-life single person who watches other couples celebrating the various family passages and knows that he or she will never share the experience; the breadwinner who faces the painful moment of a layoff and realizes that he or she wasn't important enough to be retained by the company when an economic decision had to be made.

There can be many moments of quiet pain in the afternoon of life as evidence sometimes appears to mount up that we've not made the difference we wanted to make. A child of ours breaks relationship with us, and we are tempted to assume that we have not succeeded as parents. We are passed over for a promotion; we become aware that our peers are advancing faster in life than we are; we are not selected for leadership positions that call for respect of our judgment and wisdom. When such evidence seems to move against us, there will be quiet, ponderous moments of reflection highlighting the question "What's it all about?"

Life on the tightrope engenders other sorts of questions also. Take the one that centers on what I call response. Who knows me? And who have I known? This in fact may be more of a male-oriented question than female, although—as I will point out in a minute—that too may be changing with our culture.

Carl Jung noted that in the afternoon of life there are certain "male" and "female" traits and sensitivities that seem to "rebalance" themselves in men and women. For example, within the male perspective there may be a growing urge for satisfying relationships (what he calls a female trait), an urge which did not exist within the male during the morning of life, when such a powerful force pointed toward accomplishing and establishing oneself in terms of successful functioning. Conversely, for a woman, there may be a new desire to look at life from a less relational orientation and more toward doing something different, something more measurable and capable of being tangibly rewarded. Put simply, a wage-earning male may fantasize about breaking away from his job, while a mothering female may suddenly decide to go out and seek employment. What's happening? Previously suppressed traits may be in sudden ascendance.

At mid-life the male is likely to look into himself and note feelings of loneliness. Possibly he senses that he has forfeited the opportunity to know some of his children, that he has squandered time that could have been invested in fostering a deeper relationship with his wife. He makes note of the fact that he probably doesn't have one good friend. Such feelings are intensified as he wonders who he would talk to if he faced a challenge where he would have to open up his life to someone to receive counsel or comfort.

This loneliness leads to several possible relational reactions. I've described already the pursuit of one man to enter into some sort of "affair" with a younger woman who symbolizes a flight backward to younger days when life was less complicated and more oriented toward fun or pleasure. The opposite of the pursuit of an affair is the tendency of some men to deal with their loneliness by withdrawing into a personal "cocoon," working harder, communicating less, filling hours with action rather than reflection or relationship.

But most mid-life men struggling with loneliness probably will fit in somewhere between these two extremes. Regularly they will make attempts at friendships, at a renewal of the marital relationship, at some sort of contact with their children. And the results will likely be mixed. For the others to whom they reach out are not likely to receive all the signals and understand what the male is asking for. Besides, they will have their own tracks of life that they are pursuing, and they may not have the time the other is demanding. It can be a tragic cycle of people reaching out to each other, but not at the right time in the right way; so as a result they are like darkened ships passing in the night, unaware of the life going on inside, because the doors and portholes are tightly closed.

We are seeing an interesting version of this loneliness in some women who in the sixties and seventies began to pursue a new role in society. In the pursuit of wholeness, the women's movement urged them to "Get out of the house, wife!" And for the first time since World War II, enormous numbers of women began to lay aside the traditional vocation of motherhood and enter into the labor force.

It was an impressive (though to some disturbing) movement, and in order to establish itself, it tended sometimes to hint at the idea that bearing children, maintaining a home, or even pursuing the traditional man-woman relationship was a second-class ambition. A large portion of a generation of women accepted this way of thinking and set out to pursue the "functional" life-style of the American male.

We may be in the earliest phases of discovering the results of that pursuit. Megan Marshall, for one, is suggesting that the ultimate negative result has been a loss of the female capacity for intimacy, the great strength of the female gender. In the pursuit of equality, Marshall writes, women followed the path of uniformity. And she claims it hasn't worked.

The new baby boom in the United States is marked with a large number of women in the upper thirties and early mid-life apparently trying to make up for lost time and having the children they chose not to have in earlier years.

What all of this suggests to me is that we may be seeing an

interesting need on the part of mid-life women to regain the intimacy (the relational side) they may have risked in the pursuit of functional success.

When Saint Paul spent those months in a Roman jail, there was one other issue that hung over his head—death. He knew he was no longer counting how many days he had lived, but rather how many days were left. Suddenly years of living, from childhood to adolescence to adulthood—the accomplishments, the relationships, the learning experiences—were about to be terminated. And all this was out of his control. His future would apparently be decided by others.

I call them death thoughts. Our sense of mortality, easily ignored in earlier days of the morning of life, becomes a looming reality as years pass. Our son turns twenty, and I say to my wife, "It seems as if it were yesterday that he was born. Where have the twenty years gone?" Then a second thought brushes past the mind: *The next twenty will go even faster*—and beyond that, the increasing chances of life's termination. Sensation, relation, accumulation . . . gone, over.

The words elude the mind's comprehension of death. One can only think of limits and ends, losses and weaknesses. There is increasing sensitivity to the state of old people whose feebleness and vulnerability become increasingly apparent. One fears someday becoming one of these. Awareness grows that there will come a loss of power and control. *Loss, loss, loss*—the thought strikes the soul. And the response of some? Bitterness, fear, avoidance.

But there are alternative views. The difference depends upon whether or not one chooses to develop spiritual thinking, like Abraham, or nonspiritual thinking, as did his nephew, Lot.

Paul of Tarsus grasps the prison bars. *On what day shall my life end? And of what significance can these days be? Who cares whether or not I am here or what I do?* The questions surge in his mind. And what he writes to the Philippians tells us something of how he handles himself. For there are answers to his questions; he knows them well, and they have made all the difference.

Paul will not fall from his high wire. And those who are in lockstep with him will not be betrayed. The trip he began, he will finish. "I have fought a good fight," he writes to his young partner in ministry, "I have finished my course" (2 Timothy 4:7 KJV). But behind these assertions is the fact that he has done his homework. Paul understands how to think spiritually.

"Ich kahn nicht mehr halten." I cannot hold on any longer— the pressure of life on the high wire, where the crowd looks on and the people with whom one works and lives depend upon a systematic and predictable performance. How we not only hold on but walk purposefully to the other end of the wire depends largely on the state of that inner world, the spirit to which God speaks with words of hope, direction, and personal affirmation.

14
Walking Tall
on the Wire

I have great feeling for the man on the tightrope, who suddenly caved in. I appreciate the mixture of fear and fatigue that must have shaken his body in the seconds before he cried out, *"Ich kahn nicht mehr halten."* For I, too, have toed my way across the wire, and I understand the numbness that can overcome the mind and the emotions and make one suddenly want to cry out, "I can't hold on any longer, either." A potential loss of heart is not an unknown experience.

I understand the odd urge to let myself slip, even if it would mean danger to others with whom I share the walk across the wire. I'm not unaware of the feeling that others behind me and before me can make this walk much better than I can, so I have been tempted sometimes to ask, "Why try to keep up with them?" Finally, I'm not oblivious to the eyes of the onlooking crowd, which occasionally focus upon me and quietly question whether or not I have it in me to make it to the other end.

No reflective person living through the afternoon of life will avoid these sorts of feelings at one time or another. It is not necessary that one fail or even come near to failure to experience the taunts and temptations of inward doubt or despair. Many of us will have to live with them as we inch our way across the high wire.

Even the great men and women of history were not immune to the circumstances that could threaten stability while walking at great heights. Saint Paul, on his wire, wrestled with personal issues that are real, even today, to anyone in the afternoon of life.

Take for example the matter of trappedness. Talk about trappedness in life, and one conjures up something like a jail. Paul's entrapment was a literal jail. How was he going to handle the situation?

A lot of his handling of the matter began with his attitude.

> Two men look out through the same bars
> One sees mud, and one the stars.

Paul saw stars. Attitude! Positive and opportunistic. He looked about him and concluded that jails can become anything you want them to be. He made his prison a center point for world evangelization.

Noting that soldiers from the elite troops of the Caesar were assigned to supervise his internment, Paul spent time sharing his personal faith with them. Who better to introduce to his God and then to challenge with the notion of pressing the Christian gospel into every nook and cranny of the Roman empire?

The soldiers who became Paul's congregation were tomorrow's officers and leaders. They would journey throughout the empire on the Caesar's travel bill. Their influence would be felt in the highest places. They thought they'd come to Paul's jail to keep him under guard. But because of his attitude, they became the prisoners instead, Paul the free man. He refused to allow circumstances become a prison.

Doubtless some slaves touched Paul's life as he spent his time in incarceration. Like the soldiers, they had access to the palace of the Caesar. We know that for a fact, because their Christian symbols and slogans adorn the walls of the hallways of Nero's excavated palace. Did Paul have a direct effect on things like that? Most certainly!

It is likely that Paul had greater success as a jailbird, in terms of his overall objective of world evangelism, than when he was out on his own, traveling from place to place. In jail he had the time and opportunity to train men; in jail he had time to pen some of the most significant letters of the New Testament. Saint Paul saw the stars.

When we are living at high noon, we make a choice. Is our world to be a jail or a launching pad? Paul chose the latter. Too many are tempted to see the former.

If we see our life as entrapment, we are tempted to surround it with all sorts of sensation: experiences on the periphery, which we hope will add color to what we perceive as a colorless life. Instead of enjoying the weekdays, we live for the weekend. Rather than developing the marriage relationship, we are tempted to take chances for a few exciting minutes in a clandestine relationship. We are in jail, so we seek escape.

Paul never sought escape. But he didn't accept the normal limits of his jail either. As he wrote to his friends, ". . . The things which have happened to me have served to advance the gospel so that my bonds (limitations) in Christ have become manifest in the palace and in all other places . . ." (*see* Philippians 1:12, 13). Here is a man with an attitude, who may occasionally slip, but who is not likely to fall.

Neither was Paul overly upset when it came to competition. He knew some people beyond the jail saw his imprisonment as more limiting than he did. They perceived it as a time to wrest leadership and influence from Paul, while he was out of circulation. And they tried hard. A smaller-thinking person with a negative attitude would have turned bitter and struggled with this antagonistic behavior. But not Paul. Rather he saw what others would have called competition as a cause for rejoicing. At least, he observed at one point, people were out doing something for the gospel, and that was much better than having nothing happen. It was all in his attitude.

Finally, when it came to facing the possibility of death by execution, one does not sense any hint of Paul cowering in fear or panic. His performance is marked by calmness, a tranquility built on an understanding of death not as a termination of human experience or as a defeat or as a loss of personal control, but as an opportunity to expand the horizons of reality. Death is not a "win or lose" matter; rather it is an open door. There are opportunities to be seized, Paul writes to his friends, whether one lives or dies.

You could say that Paul was ready for anything, not surprised by anything. No circumstance would be permitted to limit his style, alter his convictions, or derail his sense of life's purpose.

Paul's perspective seems to be the major secret for anyone on a high wire, where danger abounds and the consequences of failure are great. And his perspective is controlled by his attitude.

Attitude is the great watershed for those living at high noon. If the circumstances, the culture, and the process of aging are permitted to shape our attitudes, then a slip from the wire becomes inevitable. But if the opposite is true, that our attitudes speak to the environment about us, then a new, re-created life at high noon is a distinct possibility. And that is specifically a spiritual decision. William James said: "The greatest revolution in our generation is the discovery that human beings, by changing the inner attitudes of their minds, can change the outer aspects of their lives."

Many have reflected upon the observations of psychiatrist Viktor Frankl, who, as a prisoner in a Nazi concentration camp, studied the behavior of fellow prisoners during World War II. What, he set out to discover, separated the survivors from those who—to use our metaphor—could not hold on any longer, who gave up and died? Simply put: *attitude!* The ability to form an inner world that was oblivious to circumstances and pressures in the outer world and then to press the effects of the inner life into the outer world.

> We who lived in concentration camps can remember the men who walked through the huts comforting others, giving away their last piece of bread. They may have been few in number, but they offer proof that everything can be taken from a man but one thing: the last of the human freedoms—to choose one's attitude in any given set of circumstances, to choose one's own way.
> And there are always choices to make. Every day, every hour, offered the opportunity to make a decision, a decision which determined whether you would or would not submit to those powers which threatened to rob you of your very self, your inner freedom; which determined whether or not you would become the plaything of circumstance, renouncing freedom and dignity to become molded into the form of the typical inmate.
> ... Even though conditions such as lack of sleep, insufficient food and various mental stresses may suggest that the inmates were bound to react in certain ways, in the final analysis it becomes clear that the sort of person the prisoner became was the result of an inner decision, and not the result of camp influences alone. Fundamentally, therefore, any man can, even under such circumstances, decide what shall become of him—mentally and spiritually.

What is the source of such a triumphant attitude that denies the paralysis often caused by feelings of entrapment, overwhelming competition, and death? The answer Paul would give would focus upon his chosen objective in life: not a financial objective or a professional one—rather a spiritual objective formed and fostered *within* personal experience, not without. He would call it a relationship with and a commitment to Jesus Christ. And that is where spiritual thinking begins.

When a person thinks spiritually, all sorts of issues take on a new viewpoint. From Paul's vantage point, for example, the jail provided a unique opportunity to present his view of Christ to the nations. The competition mounted by "friends" only meant that more people were preaching Christ on the streets of Rome. His own possible death simply meant that he would get to see Christ sooner. With such a strong spiritual center, there was not an issue or an incident big enough in the outer world that could negatively affect him.

Malcolm Muggeridge speaks from the same perspective in our day when he says to David Porter in an interview:

> I may, I suppose, regard myself or pass for being a relatively successful man. People occasionally stare at me in the streets—that's fame. I can fairly easily earn enough to qualify for admission to the higher slopes of the Internal Revenue—that's success. Furnished with money and a little fame even the elderly, if they care to, may partake of trendy diversions—that's pleasure. It might happen once in a while that something I said or wrote was sufficiently heeded for me to persuade myself that it represented a serious impact on our time—that's fulfillment. Yet I say to you—and I beg you to believe me—multiply these tiny triumphs by a million, add them all together, and they are nothing—less than nothing, a positive impediment—measured against one draught of that living water Christ offers to the spiritually thirsty, irrespective of who or what they are.

Frighteningly, at high noon the wire we are walking on seems to be getting higher and the consequences of slipping greater. The possibility of loss grows greater, while the time to

perfect the walk grows shorter. Add to this the growing awareness on the part of a lot of mid-lifers that targets we set, the
props we elected to use, and the rewards we thought worthwhile suddenly appear to become frightfully unreliable and of
questionable value.

It is a natural time to switch from outer, more materialistic,
thinking to spiritual or inward-directed thinking, such as the
kind Paul employed. And his began with Christ. The more I
have walked through life at high noon, the more significant
this switch from outer thinking to inner, spiritual thinking has
become. And that switch is an ever-present possibility for men
and women at noon in their lives.

I began this book with a reflection upon a basketball game
where men surged up and down a basketball court, playing
their hearts out in an attempt to prove that agility and capabil-
ity meant they were still young and spirited. Looking back, I
realize that there was a time when I tried to play a different sort
of game in much the same way. I was the genuine outer-world
thinker.

Like many, I came into adulthood with many natural talents
and capacities. They afforded me a fast beginning to my chosen vocation, and before I had reached my thirties, there was
the general feeling on my part and those about me that I would
enjoy an effective life as a pastor and preacher. But what I did
not fully appreciate in those early days was the same thing the
men on the basketball court found hard to face: Natural talents
alone cannot maintain the momentum of life. They provide
quick starts, but not long-range endurance.

While such abilities may provide an impressive beginning,
the conclusion may not be so wonderful. Two quarters of good
basketball are not enough. The game is four quarters long.
And that was the trouble with the beleaguered older men in
that game. They faded quickly in the third quarter. Skill was
not enough.

Looking back, I now realize that I made an important discovery about life just in time. Had I not done so, mid-life

would have meant many slips and a probable fall. I discovered the serious matter of developing the inner world.

Saint Paul had warned his Corinthian friends that the outer person (the body and natural skills) were wasting away. The important matter, he said, was the development of the inner person, wherein one hears the voice of God and gathers in the endurance and desire to make it across the wire.

My reading of the mystics (the explorers of inner space) convinced me that, like Paul, they were on to something. For they experimented with and discovered the significance of developing the spirit. And with that development came the key to breaking the hold on something called the mid-life crises.

Discovering the importance of moving from dependence upon external systems of life to the nurturing of the inner space became the most important single insight of my preafternoon life. For while things might be changing with consistency in the outer world, there could be, I found, a serenity, a stability, and a sense of inner direction could be established through a regular, disciplined pursuit of God's presence.

The failure to regard this inner spiritual exercise is at the base of a hundred lesser struggles in mid-life. Because we do not first establish our existence at this point, we are left to define our existence out in the external areas of our lives, where we are at the mercy of opinions, fads, pressures, and persuasions.

No wonder the mid-lifer on the high wire wavers and stumbles when his spiritual equilibrium is not properly balanced. He trusts in the energies, the charisma, the sensations that so often made the past an exciting experience. But slowly they dissipate, and without an adequate inner world, little equilibrium, little fuel, and little impetus remain to keep him pressing for the other end of the wire. Feet begin to slip, and one day the cry is heard, "I can't hold on any longer!"

The development of inner space begins with a quiet commitment to God that remains to this day so simple that it defies both the egos and the logic of modern-thinking people. It is a conversion of sorts from an ego-directed life and value system to a Christ-directed one. Stumbles and falterings may mark it, but no fatal slips.

When Saint Peter first encountered the possibility of such a relationship, he was genuinely frightened and said so. Christ's answer, "Do not be afraid. . . ." Slowly Peter lost his fear, and despite his tendency to slip with frequency, he never fell to his destruction. When others faded from the scene at the noon of their lives, Peter picked up speed and reached the other end of his wire.

Peter never walked a high wire, but he did make an attempt to walk on water and did a fairly credible job of it, as long as he kept his eyes upon Christ, the destination point of his walk. But when he grew fearful and lowered the eyes, he began to slip. His *"Ich kahn nicht mehr halten"* came out as "Help me!" And the arm of Christ was extended to provide the necessary stabilizing force.

One wishes the man on the high wire in Detroit could have had such a hand reaching out to him at his terrible moment. We do at the midpoint of our walk on the wire. Christ becomes, to the person who commits to Him, an inner equilibrium, an outer balancing prop, a point toward which to walk. With that sort of stabilization, no mid-lifer ever need fear the possibility of a slip. One can hold on longer and longer, because one is held—by God.

Epilogue
Am I Really Alive?

Living at high noon is a challenge, an opportunity, an adventure. Bodies, vocations, relationships, and spirit: All enter a state of change. But in which direction? Toward what end?

Many have been fond of quoting Henry David Thoreau, who spent part of his nineteenth-century life in Walden Woods, not far from where I live. When asked to explain why he sought isolation, he said:

> I went to the woods because I wished to live deliberately, to front only the essential facts of life, and see if I could not learn what it had to teach, and not, when I came to die, discover that I had not lived.

At the high noon of life, more than a few of us might feel tempted to pursue an escape fantasy and run for the woods. But chances are we can't and wouldn't anyway. But even if we can't head for the woods, we may find that mid-life is a time to discover whether or not we are really living. The noon of life may provide the exciting potential to find out who we really are.

Dreams, fantasies, and ambitions may still remain a legitimate part of life, but now we may understand where all of life is leading and where this course may take us. Some of us will like the answers; others of us will not. And if we're among the latter, there is time and opportunity to make the necessary mid-course corrections.

The tendency of all who discuss life at high noon is to look at it from a problem-solving perspective. That means we focus in on the struggles and often do it at the expense of reflecting upon the mid-life joys. Perhaps we create previously non-existent burdens in the minds of one another. If so, that is regrettable.

But life at noon has every promise of new starts and accelerated possibilities for our relationships and our spirits. It is a time when a man or woman can ask new questions about what it means to know others and to know God. And all this we may pursue in a relaxed frame of mind, in a context where the need to visibly succeed or acquire is considerably diminished.

This book of mid-life reflections has wandered about through problem and possibility. I've not restrained myself from being personally vulnerable, from raising questions for which I had no apparent answers. Other writers will have the data, the research, the clinical treatments for middle life. For me the reflections are enough. Too much investigation will rob the entire process of living of its mystery. Study a rose, petal by petal, and when you have finished its dissection, you will understand the structure of a rose, but you will no longer have one to enjoy. I feel like that about my mid-life when it gets too close to the scrutiny of the experts.

The longer I wrote about middle life, the more I realized what I was leaving out. The more I saw of possible exceptions to every point. The more I came to appreciate the differences in people and their responses to the world about them. But of one thing I became sure. Mid-life without an inner center point is a life without direction. It is, to borrow from my son and daughter's vocabulary, a drag. But mid-life with a center point is an opportunity for personal growth and achievement.

A center point is a place from which all measurements are taken: the measure of distance covered (progress), the measure of change and growth (quality), the measure of service (contribution). The center point never changes; it remains constant. It is not affected by outside forces, by changes, by the passage of the years.

No center point comes nearer to the possibilities of which I speak than that provided by Jesus Christ. My commitment to Him grows increasingly firm; my desire to be like Him increasingly intense. And because I have now come to see the faults and flaws in my young-adult energy and fantasy, it is all the easier today to call Him Lord.

Christ first made the offer of being a center point to His disciples. "Follow Me," He told them, "and I will make you into something special." To others He made the same claim in different words: trust in Me; believe in Me; accept Me. In spiritual terminology, His was an invitation to discipleship. And those who accepted the invitation became different, better people.

As their center point, He became the measurement for all truth, for all choices, for the formation of all values, for the quality of all relationships, for their expectations and aspirations concerning the future. But it began with a commitment. They had to change direction and follow Him.

In our time no one has illustrated this commitment better than Charles Colson, former special assistant to President Nixon, during the Watergate era. Colson's story of power and achievement is well-known. His life in the corridors of White House power symbolized virtually everything that most of us desire out of life, whether we are speaking of our public worlds or our private lives. Like the Colson of those days, we, too, dream of being successful, significant, and certainly happy.

But for Charles Colson there came a disillusioning fall from the top, the loss of privilege, the humiliation of federal prison. And what came out of it? An opportunity to make things new.

It emerged through his conversion experience to a new life under the direction of Christ.

Colson tells of the moment it began to happen. In his book *Born Again,* he recalls sitting in his automobile, thinking back across the evening hours and a conversation with his close friend Tom Phillips, who had talked about the meaning of following Christ. Suddenly things had begun to make sense to him:

> With my face cupped in my hands, head leaning forward against the wheel, I forgot about machismo, about pretenses, about fears of being weak. And as I did, I began to experience a wonderful feeling of being released. Then came the strange sensation that water was not only running down my cheeks, but surging through my whole body as well, cleansing and cooling as it went. They weren't tears of sadness and remorse, nor of joy—but somehow, tears of relief.
>
> And then I prayed my first real prayer. "God, I don't know how to find You, but I'm going to try! I'm not much the way I am now, but somehow I want to give myself to You." I didn't know how to say more, so I repeated over and over the words: *Take me.*
>
> I had not "accepted" Christ—I still didn't know who He was. My mind told me it was important to find that out first, to be sure that I knew what I was doing, that I meant it and would stay with it. Only, that night, something inside me was urging me to surrender—to what or to whom I did not know.
>
> I stayed there in the car, wet-eyed, praying, thinking, for perhaps half an hour, perhaps longer, alone in the quiet of the dark night. Yet for the first time in my life I was not alone at all.

The result? An incredible change of life that today benefits a large number of men and women who have hit the bottom of the prisons of the world. The hatchet man of the Nixon administration like the hatchet man of organized religion 2,000 years ago—Saul of Tarsus—found a new center point. It's an experience we all need.

When I left a basketball game between a group of young boys and aging men a few years ago, I knew that what I'd seen was more than a game. It was part of a drama repeated in each generation. A few good men were telling on themselves. To be sure they enjoyed the competitive encounter, but they were also out to prove that they were perpetually young. And they failed. They were pursuing the wrong objective, in the wrong place, against the wrong opponents. And I was as guilty as they were. Living at high noon deserves better than that. Youthfulness should not have been the goal. Maturity is the better pursuit. And that in fact can come at high noon. The reaching of its potential lies beyond the gym door, out in the real world, and that is where I headed.

> Lord God, here I am at the noon of life.
> Never having been here before,
> I admit to being scared
> about the unfamiliar ground.
>
> I worry too much Lord—
>   about failing
>   about missing out
>   about being passed up
>   about weakness
>   about dying
>   about security.
>
> Lord God, here I am at the noon of life.
> Never having been here before,
> I admit to needing You
> To lead me over the unfamiliar ground.
> To remind me that it can be okay.

I lean on You, Lord, to help me—
    become effective as a person
    trust Your opinions rather than
        those of others
    accept my honest limits
    prepare for eternity
    love my wife
    be a good friend
    value integrity
    and find security in
        the pursuit of maturity.

AN INTRODUCTION TO DRAMA

THE MACMILLAN COMPANY
NEW YORK · BOSTON · CHICAGO · DALLAS
ATLANTA · SAN FRANCISCO

MACMILLAN AND CO., Limited
LONDON · BOMBAY · CALCUTTA · MADRAS
MELBOURNE

THE MACMILLAN COMPANY
OF CANADA, Limited
TORONTO

AN INTRODUCTION TO
DRAMA

BY

JAY B. HUBBELL, Ph.D.
PROFESSOR OF ENGLISH IN DUKE
UNIVERSITY

AND

JOHN O. BEATY, Ph.D.
PROFESSOR OF ENGLISH IN SOUTHERN
METHODIST UNIVERSITY

Corrected First Edition, With Index

New York
THE MACMILLAN COMPANY

7539

To
L. S. H.
AND
J. P. B.

PREFACE

An Introduction to Drama is intended primarily for college classes. It is planned for courses in types of literature and for advanced courses beginning a systematic study of the drama. For playgoers, and for the increasing body of people who read plays, it will furnish an opportunity for becoming acquainted with the principles and the progress of the drama.

The twenty-nine complete plays represent nearly every type which has been important in England and America together with certain foreign types which directly or through dramatic criticism have exerted considerable influence on the drama in English. For the inclusion and discussion of foreign plays we have no apology. The drama of western Europe has been increasingly international. From the tropes and miracle plays to the current popular successes, plays have been moved from country to country. Surely Sophocles, Plautus, Molière, and Ibsen are important names in a history of English drama.

The omission of plays by Shakespeare, on the other hand, has for several reasons seemed desirable. In the first place, high schools differ considerably in the choice of plays for special study; and it must be deemed unwise for an elementary college text to repeat plays which have already been studied intensively by some of the pupils. Again, to give Shakespeare proper representation would have expanded an already large book. And, finally, the plays of Shakespeare are universally available in cheap editions of sufficient variety and merit to afford every teacher a suitable list of plays.

In the field of dramatic history and criticism, we have attempted the difficult task of condensing into ten short chapters a body of fact which is usually treated under many heads. We have, in the main, selected plays of high literary quality, but we have considered them less as "mere literature" than as acting drama. In consequence, we have included an opera and have treated the history of the spectacle and the play with music. We have not only woven the story of English drama into its continental background; we have also tried to describe the stage and the theatrical conditions of each period and to show how authors, actors, and managers have been influenced by the life of the time.

In deference to the suggestions of the great majority of the teachers with whom we have consulted, we have omitted detailed comment and critical notes upon the plays included. Over-edited texts force the teacher into the embarrassing dilemma of repeating the textbook or of discussing relatively trivial points.

The dates given in parentheses after the titles of plays refer to the date of production except when they are printed in italics; in the latter case the date of publication is given.

In the difficult task of selection and criticism, we have exercised our own judgment whenever possible, but in many cases we have been guided by the advice of others. We owe a general obligation to most of the works listed in the Bibliography. Professors George Pierce Baker, of Yale University; Brander Matthews, of Columbia University; and David H. Stevens, of the University of Chicago; and President William Allan Neilson, of Smith College, have kindly reviewed and criticized our plan and our choice of plays. In certain matters we have sought the advice of Messrs. Joseph Wood Krutch, W. E. Schultz, Curtis Hidden Page, Emery Neff, and Oral S. Coad. We are also indebted to our colleagues on the English staff of Southern Methodist University and to certain of our colleagues in other departments, especially Miss Dorothy Amann and Professors C. Franklyn Zeek and John S. McIntosh. Many of the living authors of included plays have added a critical or an encouraging word in sending their approval of our use of their work. Mr. Barrett H. Clark has revised his translation of Tchekoff's *The Boor* for this collection. To all these men and women we extend our thanks, and we absolve them from all responsibility for the errors of fact and judgment which must inevitably appear in a survey of so extended a field. We wish to thank Mr. R. R. Smith and Mr. L. W. Lamm of the Macmillan Company for much helpful advice and assistance in seeing the book through the press. For assistance in the onerous task of preparing the manuscript for the press, we wish to express our especial gratitude to the following assistants in the Department of English: Miss Ruby Mae Harbin, Miss Eunice Brooks, Miss Sarah Chokla, and Miss Mary Lamar.

The plan of *An Introduction to Drama* was conceived by Mr. Beaty. Mr. Hubbell wrote Chapters I, II, IV, IX, and X; Mr. Beaty wrote Chapters III, V, VI, VII, and VIII. Each author, however, has revised the chapters written by the other, and each accepts responsibility for the entire book.

J. B. H.
J. O. B.

Southern Methodist University,
Dallas, Texas,
April, 1927.

PREFACE TO CORRECTED FIRST EDITION, WITH INDEX

A few errors were corrected in the second printing and others have been corrected in the fourth. We wish to express our great thanks to Miss Mary Lamar for making the index which has been added to this printing.

J. B. H.
J. O. B.

September, 1929.

ACKNOWLEDGMENTS

The generous co-operation of playwrights, translators, and publishers has made possible the inclusion of a number of plays which are still in copyright. We wish to express our grateful obligation to those authors, editors, translators, and other persons who have added their permission to that of their publishers: Miss Alice Gerstenberg, Lord Dunsany, Sir Arthur Wing Pinero, President William Allan Neilson, Professors Edward Capps, Frederick H. Koch, and Curtis Hidden Page, Messrs. Barrett H. Clark, Henry Arthur Jones, and Eugene O'Neill. To the following publishers and other persons we are indebted for permission to reprint copyrighted material:

BONI AND LIVERIGHT—
For Eugene O'Neill's *The Emperor Jones.*

BRENTANO'S—
For Alice Gerstenberg's *Overtones.*

THE CAMBRIDGE UNIVERSITY PRESS—
For Sir Richard Claverhouse Jebb's translation of Sophocles' *Antigone.*

CHARLES SCRIBNER'S SONS—
For William Archer's translation of Ibsen's *A Doll's House.*

SAMUEL FRENCH—
For Barrett H. Clark's translation of Tchekoff's *The Boor.*

WILLIAM HEINEMANN, LTD., THE WALTER H. BAKER COMPANY, AND SIR ARTHUR WING PINERO—
For Pinero's *The Second Mrs. Tanqueray.*

HENRY HOLT AND COMPANY—
For Harold Williamson's *Peggy.*

THE HOUGHTON MIFFLIN COMPANY—
For the Neilson text of Marlowe's *Doctor Faustus,* Jonson's *Volpone,* and Beaumont and Fletcher's *Philaster.*

B. W. HUEBSCH AND THE VIKING PRESS—
For Charles Henry Meltzer's translation of Gerhart Hauptmann's *The Assumption of Hannele.*

MR. HENRY ARTHUR JONES—
For his *The Goal.*

MR. JAMES LOEB—
For Paul Nixon's translation of Plautus's *Menæchmi.*

JOHN W. LUCE AND COMPANY—
For Synge's *Riders to the Sea.*

THE MACMILLAN COMPANY—
For Henderson Daingerfield Norman's translation of Rostand's *Cyrano de Bergerac* and William Butler Yeats's *The Land of Heart's Desire* (by arrangement with A. P. Watt & Co.).

THE MODERN LIBRARY, INC.—
For the translation of Maeterlinck's *The Intruder.*

G. P. PUTNAM'S SONS—
For Dunsany's *A Night at an Inn* and Curtis Hidden Page's translation of Molière's *Tartuffe.*

SMALL, MAYNARD AND COMPANY—
For Susan Glaspell's *Trifles.*

PROFESSORS JOHN S. P. TATLOCK AND ROBERT G. MARTIN—
For the modernized versions of *The Second Shepherds' Play* and the Brome *Abraham and Isaac* found in their *Representative English Plays* (the Century Company).

CONTENTS

AN INTRODUCTION TO DRAMA